WHO AM I?

An A - Z Career Guide for Teens

Tai Abrams

Check out another book by Tai Abrams called:

The Money Mastery Project
Coming Soon

to learn more about how she paid off $143,000 of undergraduate student loans and how you can position yourself for financial independence.

WHO AM I?

An A-Z Career Guide for Teens

Tai Abrams

2017

WHO AM I?

An A - Z Career Guide for Teens
By: Tai Abrams

ISBN: 978-0-9987413-0-7
Library of Congress Control Number: 2017902589

Because of the dynamic nature of the internet, any web addresses or links contained in this book may have changed since publication and may no longer be valid. The views expressed in this book are solely those of the author and do not necessarily reflect the views of the publisher, and the publisher hereby disclaims any responsibility for them.

Salary information taken from the Bureau of Labor Statistics.

Any cartoon illustrations included in and on this book was completed on Fiverr.com. Commercial use has been paid for and granted.

Edited by The Muse and the Messenger, LLC
Cartoon Illustrations by Triper1410, Book Cover Design by Galesackss
Author photo by Daniel Ortiz

RPT Enterprises creates books, games and other educational resources to help learners of all ages Realize Potential Totally. These books and resources are available at special discounts when purchased in bulk for premiums and sales promotions as well as for fund-raising or educational use. Special editions can also be created to specifications. For details, contact the Special Sales Director at the following email address: sales@TaiAbrams.com

Printed in the United States of America
First printing June 2017

Dedication

I dedicate this book to my mom, Patricia Abrams, who always set the bar of excellence so high that I had no choice but to shoot for the stars. I love you with all my heart. To my Goddess mother and mentor Fortunio Slocombe, thank you for speaking the favor of God into and over my life and teaching me how to move more deeply into my walk of faith in Jesus Christ. I AM overjoyed that God blessed me with your love. You two women have supported and inspired me to heal the wound, restore the family and build the nation. I extend my deepest love and gratitude to you both. Know that this is only the beginning.

Contents

Acknowledgements

I would like to thank God and all the angels that were sent in my path to bring this book to children all over the world. I would also like to thank my mom, Fortunio, my beloved sisters, Candice and Crystal, my dear friend Valerie, my mentors, Mr. Reid, Ms. Gathers and Wallace, my adorable niece, Camiya, my Goddess sisters, Maritza and Janet, and all those who have played a role in bringing this work to life. Thank you for your support, patience, guidance, and valuable suggestions. You helped me to see this project all the way through by holding me accountable. You believe in my vision to transform the children of today into the leaders and innovators of tomorrow. Without your support, this book would not exist. You all mean the world to me and the children will be blessed because you believe in me and in their potential. Shoutout to the current students, alumni, parents, friends, past employees and supporters of my company, AdmissionSquad, Inc.! I love you all so much and I wish you the greatest success in life. May this book be a blessing to all of you! Keep winning and dreaming BIG darlings.

Call & Response

⎡ Who Am I?
⎢ I declare: I AM Somebody   **Repeat 4 Times**
⎣ Response: Somebody GREAT! ⎤

I AM a/an [insert career choice 1 here] Response: Yeah!!!
I AM a/an [insert career choice 2 here] Response: Yeah!!!
I AM a/an [insert career choice 3 here] Response: Yeah!!!
And I won't be stopped.
No he/she won't be stopped. Yeah!!!

[REPEAT initial declaration 4 times]

I AM [insert character trait 1 here] Response: Yeah!!!
I AM [insert character trait 2 here] Response: Yeah!!!
I AM [insert character trait 3 here] Response: Yeah!!!
And I won't give up.
No he/she won't give up. Yeah!!!

[REPEAT initial declaration 4 times]

This book is a gift for:

because I care about you deeply and I want you to be successful.

1. INTRODUCTION

Welcome to one of the most exciting journeys of your life. The journey toward ultimate success and an exceptional career. One of the biggest myths is that college preparation begins in your junior year of high school and career development begins in your junior year of college. Sorry to bust that myth, but college preparation and career development should begin before you even leave middle school. Yes, the truth is students should begin thinking about and exploring their options for future academic and career success long before preparing for the Scholastic Assessment Test (SAT), American College Test (ACT), or completing college applications. Actually, students should begin identifying and weighing their options long before the guidance counselor reminds them to do so, which may not always happen in cases where counselors are overextended. Unfortunately, many students and parents, alike, lack the necessary education and knowledge to prepare adequately for this pivotal time and often fail to do so in a manner that presents the best possible outcome. The good news is I am not just here to be a myth buster. I am here to offer my personal experiences and success story to help students who are in middle and high school navigate the overwhelming and unpredictable process of journeying toward success. The journey toward ultimate success is not easy, but this resource guide is designed to support you through the daunting task of understanding the steps it takes to reach your full potential. Throughout this guide, I will serve as your personal mentor and success coach, where my primary objective is to help you realize your full potential, by helping you to discover your passions and harness your strengths. By the end, I hope to cultivate a mindset of innovation and creative problem solving so you may be in a position to change the world.

To begin with, one of the most critical steps during the success journey is identifying the real you. Some people go through life without recognizing who they are, which leaves them wandering, wasting precious time that could be put towards something more meaningful and valuable—like creating the life they want, as opposed to settling for the life someone else prescribed for them. When you know who you are and what you really want out of life, you will not waste your time focusing on things that are not at the core of your divine purpose. From a very early age, I was taught by my grandmother how important it was to build a strong relationship with God as a foundation for life success. It is through my prayer time with God over the years that I gained clarity around my purpose and have developed a deeper understanding of who I am and all that is destined for my life. Clarity of who you are will grant you an unshakable confidence and a high degree of personal power, that will allow you to achieve monumental success at a young age, like me. Once you get on the path to realizing your full potential, your life will become a dream actualized.

As your success coach, I believe that we must begin your journey by answering the question, "Who am I?" You will notice that this question is much bigger than you thought. Throughout life you will have influencers like family, friends, teachers, and social and cultural experiences all around you that will ultimately help shape who you will become. These influencers can affect your thinking, self-esteem, and decisions in many ways. By asking the question, "Who am I?" and proactively seeking the answer, you can be more deliberate about how your influencers should impact your life so you can transform into the person you see yourself being in your dreams. Becoming firm in who you are and how you want to stand in the world is made up of a variety of aspects that will determine the quality of life you experience on this earth. This book will serve as a starting point for you to learn how to have this important conversation with yourself and with God, often.

"Who am I?" is one of the most important questions that you will ask yourself, continually, as you evolve into adulthood. At times, there may be a disparity between who you see yourself as (the dream) and who you are right now (the reality). For instance, your dream may include becoming a successful real estate investor, while your reality may be that you do not even have enough money to buy a new pair of shoes. I encourage you to hold onto your vision with strength, passion, and willpower. Who you think you are is all that really matters . . . so envision yourself as the completed, final draft of yourself. Once you establish a clear vision of who you want to be, it is vital that you spend every single day moving and aggressively working toward the fulfillment of your vision. With a lot of hard work, dedication and prayer, one day you will wake up and notice that you have transformed and all your dreams have come true.

I have learned that the more you know, the faster your grow.

As cliché as it sounds, knowledge really is power. However, applied knowledge sets you up to win big in life. Likewise, this guide is a starting point and is meant to help you to begin exploring your career options before going to college. Once you know what is possible, you can start to dream on an even deeper level. But first, to help you avoid some of my biggest mistakes, I will use my personal story to help guide you toward success and expand your awareness so you can have more options available to you than I did. While reading, I encourage you to take notes along the way, consistently imagine your ideal life, dream big and take action even after closing the book. Now, it is time to leverage my journey to jumpstart your future! I pray that this book expands your thinking to miraculous, supernatural levels so you can lead a positive, fulfilling, and transformative life.

2. MY STORY

I was born into a two-parent, Guyanese American household, with two sisters—one older and one younger. Unfortunately, my parents divorced when I was three, leaving my mom, with the sole responsibility of providing for the three of us. With only an Associate degree, a job paying a measly $24,000 a year and three daughters, ages 1, 3, and 9, she was challenged with figuring out how we were going to survive. I thank God for her because she chose to be a victor and not a victim. She made major sacrifices to build a career in the healthcare industry that would allow her to fulfill her passion and reach a place of financial stability. She rose through the ranks as a registered nurse and is currently a dynamic leader overseeing large teams of healthcare professionals in New York City (NYC). She was my first example of how important it is to maintain a certain level of integrity in any situation. She also helped me realize how important it is to leverage my adversities in a way that allows my greatness to shine. However, like her, you will learn that there is a pro and a con for almost every situation. As a single mom, she spent most of her time at work and at school, so she could gain upward mobility and advance in her career. Naturally, she was not able to be around much to help us navigate our careers and figure out how to thrive in the American education system at the higher levels. We were basically latchkey kids. Thankfully, my grandparents were a great support system to me, my mom and sisters. We spent a lot of time with them in elementary and middle school to give my mother the freedom to grow her career.

With a mother who spent most of her time at work, an absentee father, and Guyanese grandparents who only had a high school education, there was little opportunity for me to gain meaningful insight about the world. My grandparents were very fearful of my sisters and I being harmed due to their traumatic childhood experiences of molestation, poverty and exploitation, so we spent much of our childhood within the confines of the family house. An over-protective parenting style left me uncertain about how to navigate the world. Needless to say, my worldview was quite limited. I did well in school but had no idea how to apply any of what

I learned or what careers were available to me in the real world. Despite my lack of worldly exposure and access to information and resources, I never stopped dreaming. I had a wild imagination that allowed me to travel to the far ends of the Earth, meet the most influential people and experience culture on my own terms. I am 100% sure that I could have figured out how to solve the world's biggest problems through my vivid imagination. I was always full of drive, ambition, resilience and a desire to lead. Books, movies, television shows, and my friends helped to expand my awareness and had a major influence on my life aspirations. I wanted to be an obstetrician, then a pediatrician, then an insurance adjuster, then the president of the United States, then an investment banker. The investment banking career goal stuck with me for quite some time. As a sophomore in college, I was so happy when I landed two internships on Wall Street at Merrill Lynch, one of the top finance companies in the world. I participated in a rotational program and learned a lot about sales & trading and investment banking[1]. This opportunity was truly one of my greatest accomplishments because I did not let my lack of exposure stop me from believing more was possible for my life. I did a great job at whatever was within my power to do—read as much as I could and did exceptionally well in school. I believed that God had a much greater plan for me.

During my middle school years, I had a phenomenal private math tutor who believed in me so much that he invested his time to help me excel two grade levels ahead of my peers in math. In seventh grade, I earned a score of 100% on the ninth-grade math regents[2]. By eighth grade, I earned a score of 98% on the tenth-grade math regents and managed to maintain the highest grade point average (GPA), allowing me to graduate from middle school in 2001 as the first class valedictorian of The Lenox Academy. My hard work paid off because I earned a qualifying score on the Specialized High School Admissions Test (SHSAT), which granted me admission into one of the top public high schools in NYC, The Bronx High School of Science. High school opened my eyes to a world of limitless possibilities because of the exceptional qualities of the school, e.g.,

[1] Investment banks help companies to raise capital to finance their projects. They also assist individuals and institutional investors with investing in projects.

[2] In New York State, Regents Examinations are statewide standardized examinations in core high school subjects required for a Regents Diploma to graduate.

high-performing students, a diverse student body, excellent teachers, over twenty advanced placement (AP) courses, access to college courses, summer internships, study abroad, and so much more! Every conversation I had with students and teachers in high school allowed me to learn something new about what the world had to offer. I was excited and started to dream even bigger. I truly believed the sky was the limit. By my senior year, I successfully completed over ten AP and honors courses, earned two college credits, competed in national math competitions, joined the oceanography team, held a job at Kaplan, and scored high on my SAT (Math: 760 Verbal: 560). I was the model student. I kept focused on my grades because something told me that school was my ticket into my dream lifestyle and career. I just knew that a high-quality education was the key to unlock the door of opportunity. I researched colleges and fell in love with and applied to Duke University, in Durham, North Carolina, one of the top five universities in the country at the time. I was elated when I was accepted. Duke University was the perfect distance from New York- far enough so I could establish my own identity and not use my mom as a crutch, but close enough so I could come home if I was ever feeling home-sick. Most of all, being accepted meant that I had a chance at creating a bigger, better, and brighter life for myself.

College offered me a sense of freedom, independence, and an opportunity to explore the world on my own terms. I was fortunate because the workload and rigor at Bronx Science adequately prepared me for Duke. Yet, despite my exceptional grades and career developmental opportunities in high school, I suffered from a bit of a learning curve. I was attending school with the children of wealthy politicians, CEO's, entrepreneurs, investment bankers, business executives, doctors, and other highly regarded, lucrative professions. Many of my peers came from two-parent households where their parents had the bandwidth to play a more active role in the professional development of their career. These students were born into networks that could grant them access to career opportunities with ease. As a freshman in college, I did not even know what a network was. My college peers had a significant advantage considering many of them were privileged. I found myself feeling insecure about the way I spoke, my lack of knowledge around current events and global politics and my less-developed vocabulary. There were times when I felt I could never catch up to all that my peers knew. Despite my freshmen year anxiety, I stayed focused on taking full advantage of the benefits of attending an elite university. I used all the resources available to me and managed to graduate with a 3.516 GPA, a Bachelor of Arts in mathematics in 2009, two internships at a top tier investment bank, a study abroad opportunity in Cairo, Egypt and a rich collegiate experience. Since then, life has been a dream. I started my career as a government consultant for Booz Allen Hamilton · in Washington, D.C. where I helped government agencies to execute their mission more effectively. On one of my projects, I was a business analytics consultant, supporting the Federal Emergency Management Agency (FEMA) to more effectively process over $3.4 billion in awarded grant funds. I built risk analysis tools to help the client to identify bottlenecks in the final stages of the award process. I was so proud of how far I had come.

Many of my career opportunities would not have crossed my path had it not been for two critical programs that literally changed my life: Sponsors for Educational Opportunity (SEO) and Management Leadership for Tomorrow (MLT). I participated in SEO during my sophomore year of college and was a part of MLT during my junior year of college. These two programs offered me the opportunity to have support in securing internships and full-time roles at Fortune 100 companies. They also provided targeted coaching on how to navigate these environments so I could be successful. I am grateful for the access SEO and MLT provided. I was so inspired by these organizations that I decided to start one of my own. After spending two years at Booz Allen Hamilton, I had a deep desire to start a company that would leave an impact on the education space. I moved back to my hometown, Brooklyn, NY, started providing private math tutoring services to students in my neighborhood and found myself becoming a champion for middle school students. It was quite common to see talented middle school students in NYC miss out on the opportunity to get into one of the top NYC public schools, like specialized high schools, like the one I attended, and other competitive screened schools, and I wanted to address this achievement gap. I teamed up with another Specialized High School graduate and got busy building a successful high school transition program, called AdmissionSquad, Inc., that would create a pipeline of students gaining admission into the city's top high schools. Our program maintained an 80% success rate of getting students into top high schools. I woke up one day and realized that I was a successful entrepreneur that was solving a pressing problem for NYC. After all the career paths that I considered, I had found my true calling as an entrepreneur. I have leveraged the leadership and business development skills that I have been blessed with to impact change across NYC and will continue to expand my reach on a global level. I have brought my God-given gifts of mathematics, public speaking, leadership and business development all over the world to places like South Africa, Panama, Ghana, Barbados, Egypt, Belize and Turkey. With all that I have accomplished, it still feels as if this is only the beginning of what God is doing in my life. My career has been quite an adventure that gets more and more exciting with each passing year. If career success was possible for me, I am certain that it is possible for you, as long as you follow the clues left behind by people who have experienced the level of success you desire.

The Secret
Learn. Think. Dream.

Here is a quick life secret. You can only attract who you are. To attract means to bring toward you with a hidden force like the pull of a magnet. If you want to be successful and leave a major impact on the world, study the greats who came before you to determine the thoughts, beliefs, actions, and networks they cultivated to achieve the kind of success you desire. To attract the career, relationships, and life of your dreams, you need to sharpen your professional tool kit to become the type of person who can handle that level of success. Every six months to a year, assess where you are and where you want to go and make a commitment to reinvent yourself into a more evolved, talented, and sharp professional. With every upgraded version of yourself, you welcome a new level of opportunity and relationships into your life. This means, it is time to make different decisions about how you are currently showing up as a student. Students who consistently turn in their homework late, talk in class, and perform horribly on exams, may attract a circle of friends whose work ethic and behavior resembles their own. But, once a low-performing student makes the decision to show up on a higher level by turning in all their assignments timely, studying for exams, and being respectful in class, they will either repel their old friends for a more focused set of friends or influence their low-performing friends to change as well. This upgrade will also welcome new opportunities in the form of internships, scholarships, and awards from teachers who have noticed this change.

One of the best things you could ever do for yourself is to establish a grand vision of who you want to be in life and spend your teenage years bringing your full vision to life. I challenge you to work overtime now to qualify yourself for opportunities when no one is looking. Even when you do not feel like you are growing, I can assure you that you are. The lessons of life are invisible but they are present. The faster you master the lessons, the faster you grow. The faster you grow, the faster you reach your destination. While your answer to the question, "Who am I?" will consistently evolve as you mature, remember that the most important element is the action you take right now to get in full alignment with the vision you see for your future. Believe that who you think you are is who you really are and go all in to bring these two into alignment. This is the start of an amazing journey! I hope you are ready.

My Biggest Obstacle: Debt

Due to my limited access to information and financial resources, I applied to Duke University, early decision, with no financial plan, and ended up with a student loan bill of $143,000. Trust me, the journey to finding a way to pay off my debt was not easy. Nonetheless, I came out on top. I am happy to say that I successfully paid off the full amount before I turned 30. Most adults carry debt with them for decades, which often hinders their ability to leverage the money earned in their chosen career to use towards building wealth. It was important for me to get to a place where debt could not hold me back from accomplishing goals like property ownership, retirement, marriage and investing in my continued professional development. While I was proud of myself for taking proactive steps toward eradicating my debt, I recognized a deeper issue centered around the minimal guidance available for first-generation families and other families where the student may be the first to matriculate into a top college. I made a commitment to share my story with those who could benefit. These tips could save you thousands of dollars if considered during the college application process. This is my gentle reminder for you to consider the cost of college because it may determine your financial success in the long term. Career success and financial success go hand in hand. Here are the pros and cons for my decision to attend Duke University to widen my career opportunities. Several points may apply to elite universities at large but can vary from school to school.

Pros	Cons
• Powerful alumni network • Basketball and great school spirit • Beautiful campus • Elite university • Increased access to lucrative internships & job opportunities • Top companies recruit on campus • Student body is full of intelligent, driven students with a desire to achieve at the highest levels • Location and weather was awesome • Located in the Research Triangle[3] • Rigorous curriculum • World-class faculty	• High tuition cost • Student loan debt is likely

I have benefited significantly from having a prestigious school like Duke University on my resume. The network that it has granted me literally changed my life. My career opportunities have certainly widened because of my Duke experience. I truly enjoyed attending my alma mater and do not regret spending my undergraduate years there. What I do regret is not being more informed about how to navigate the college admissions process and secure funding opportunities to subsidize the cost. I also wish I applied for other elite schools that would have given me more financial aid than Duke offered. Submitting several college applications would have given me a chance to negotiate with the schools to decrease my tuition cost.

How to Get into a Top College Like Me

The college/university you attend will play a significant role in your access to career opportunities. You must position yourself for

---

[3] The Research Triangle, commonly referred to as The Triangle, is located in North Carolina and includes three of the nation's top research universities: North Carolina State University, Duke University and the University of North Carolina at Chapel Hill. It is known for its highly-regarded research facilities, its consistent ability to cultivate an educated workforce and its pro-business climate. Visit www.researchtriangle.org for more information.

success in high school to widen your college options. If you want to get into a top college like I did, there are a few key steps you need to take. The college admissions application will include five critical elements:

1. **An Impressive Transcript and High Overall GPA:** Make sure you take the hardest classes available and perform with a 95 or better in each of these classes. Take as many advanced placement, honors and college level courses as are available at your high school. This will make college admissions officers see that you like to take on a challenge.

2. **High Standardized Test Scores**: You will need high scores on the SAT/ACT and SAT II subject tests. Study well in advance to qualify for scholarships.

3. **Recommendations**: Be sure to cultivate strong relationships with your teachers so you can receive excellent recommendations. You must stand out as a student for teachers to speak out on your behalf. This is where the tips in this book will become very useful.

4. **A Stand-Out Essay**: By senior year, this is the only element of your package that you will have full control over. Start writing your essay by May of your junior year and get an initial round of feedback before your summer. Work on it throughout the summer and go through 2-3 more rounds of revisions when you come back in the fall of your senior year. Remember, show, don't tell. Your story should be creative, compelling and paint an amazing picture of why you are a stand-out candidate.

5. **Extracurricular Activities/Leadership**: Get involved in activities both inside and outside of school. By junior year, you should have a leadership position in a program or club you are involved in. If your school's available options are limited, consider leading an effort in your church, your local community or a program for which you have been involved. Think outside the box if you want to stand out. There should be **one thing** that you have focused on consistently for at least five years that you are committed to mastering i.e. playing the violin, leading an initiative, student government,

competing on the debate team, etc. This level of focus and dedication will demonstrate character and is impressive to college admissions officers and scholarship committees.

Note: Some schools may require an **interview**. I am recommending that you start mastering your interview skills once you complete this book. By senior year, you should have already participated in many mock interviews to sharpen your ability to sell yourself. Do not wait until interviewing is necessary to practice. More details are included in a later chapter to get you started.

College Cost Reduction

You can find creative ways to finance your college experience. As with anything, you must plan your path appropriately to position yourself for these opportunities. Here are a few ways to reduce the cost of college:

1. Score a 4 or 5 on your Advanced placement courses to receive college credit. You will no longer be required to take these courses in college. This can allow you to save time and money and can even position you to graduate earlier.

2. Take college courses at an accredited college/university in HS.

3. Apply to no less than 100 scholarships. I know that is aggressive. I am simply letting you know what it will take to make a major dent in the cost. There are thousands of scholarships that go unclaimed every year. Create an excel document, keep track of the deadline/application requirements and apply away!

4. Get started at a less expensive school, like a community college, and then transfer into an elite school. The school you graduate from is all that matters.

5. Go to a less expensive school for undergrad and then make the investment for graduate school.

6. Become an entrepreneur to earn more money by selling your talents while in college.

7. Take the PSAT exam during your **junior year** and score amongst the top 8,000 scores (out of over 1 million students) to qualify for the automatic National Merit Scholarship. $2500 or more.

8. Land high-paying summer internships. My internships on Wall Street paid over $10,000 per summer.

9. Become a Resident Assistant (RA) to have your room and board waved.

10. Turn in your applications early before the college's financial aid budget is depleted. Be sure to apply to multiple colleges so you can negotiate your financial aid package.

Success Coach Challenge: Be an exceptional candidate, find and win multiple scholarships to eliminate the cost barrier, and apply to more schools to expand your options.

3. EXPAND YOUR AWARENESS

To gain deeper clarity around identity and life purpose, you will need to widen your horizons. Make a commitment to ask deeper questions, visit new places, meet new people, participate in more elevating experiences and interact with the world as if it is your playground to explore. I am giving you permission to be inquisitive. When you were younger, you asked your elders questions constantly to help you to understand how the world worked. Somewhere along the way, the questions may have slowed down or stopped altogether. This could have happened for a number of reasons. Despite the justification, I want you to recover that admirable characteristic so you can sharpen your mind and develop a more comprehensive definition of who you are inside of this immense world of ours. It is only by the questions that we ask that we can receive answers and truly evolve.

By reading this resource, you will learn more about the careers that are available to you. I am constantly challenging my mentees to dream big. I soon realized that you can only dream as big as you can mentally conceive. One of my students asked me, "well how can I dream big, if I don't even know what's out there?" My answer is always, "by making a commitment to be a life-long learner so you can continuously expand your realm of possibility." The fruit of this pledge is that you will never be ignorant to the possibilities. You will become an out-of-the-box thinker. There is a whole world out there that many of us are not privy to, depending on the family we are born into or the area we are from. Nonetheless, I still believe wholeheartedly that you can be and do anything you want. However, to achieve extraordinary career success, you will need to be equipped with the right tools to get there. Let this book be the catalyst for you to answer the most important question in your lifetime:

WHO AM I?

Remember, we are not defined by what we do for a living. However, what we do for a living should be a reflection of our God-given gifts. Those gifts are areas where you can be excellent! Your gifts, sometimes known as skills, have the potential to bring you so much joy when you use them in the right way. It is through your gifts that you will find freedom and perfect self-expression. Furthermore, it is through your gifts that you will be able to express fully all of who you are and who you are meant to be. Be sure to answer the question, "Who Am I?" with declarative statements that will speak to your great qualities. You will say the words, "I declare" and continue your statement with the most powerful two words you will ever encounter in your lifetime:

I AM.

The words, I AM, are the most powerful words in the whole wide world and God wants us to use these two words very wisely. You will define who you are and create your new reality by consciously selecting the words that follow, "I am." God trusts us to create a beautiful reality for ourselves by using these words with care, deep thought, and wisdom. As you expand your awareness, your response will become more colorful, broad, complex, definitive, clear and comprehensive. The definition of who you are comes through expanded awareness.

4. THE MAGIC IS IN YOUR WORDS

You may have been born into circumstances that were out of your control but there is one thing you have 100% control over every single day—your words. Your words are like the colors painted by an artist's paintbrush, and your life is the canvas. If you want to paint a beautiful picture that you can be proud of, you must choose your words very carefully. An intentional shift in the words you use will trick your brain to believe different things about your life. Your life will begin to morph into the beautiful picture you had in your head all along. Affirmations are a great tool that you can use to facilitate this process. An affirmation is a short, powerful statement that can be said, heard and thought repeatedly to adjust your life experience. I use positive affirmations to change my subconscious thoughts so I can create my new reality. Here is a great starting point:

Words to Include in Your Vocabulary

I AM successful.

I AM powerful.

I AM blessed and highly favored.

I AM a leader.

I AM innovative.

I AM intelligent.

I AM positive.

I AM confident.

I AM a lifelong learner.

I AM a dreamer and doer.

I AM a world-changer.

I AM glorious.

I AM strong.

I AM driven.

I AM focused.

I AM goal-oriented.

I AM brilliant.

I AM responsible.

I AM a winner.

I AM truth.

I AM a conqueror.

I AM passionate.

I AM love.

I AM a global citizen.

I AM great.

I AM excelling.

I AM thoughtful.

I AM willing.

I AM a college graduate.

I AM a master.

I AM beautiful.

I AM handsome.

I AM royal.

I AM joy.

I AM peace.

I AM friendship.

I AM wise.

I AM faithful.

I AM self-disciplined.

I AM divine.

I AM knowledgeable.

I AM perfect just the way I AM.

Tip: I'm is the same thing as I AM. So, this conjunction counts too!

While you are on your brand new and exciting career journey, be sure to omit statements that do not serve you and do not get you closer to your dream career and life. These words will only bring harm to your journey, and it will make it harder and less enjoyable. Avoid saying all the things you **don't** want and focus on saying all the things you **do** want. For example, instead of saying, "I don't want a teacher that gives excessive amounts of homework," you can say, "I want a teacher that gives the perfect amount of homework for me to get the practice I need." Or you can say, "I want a teacher who is considerate of my work load in my other classes when he/she assigns homework." Here are a few statements to get rid of:

Words to Exclude from Your Vocabulary

I can't.

I AM just not good at that.

I AM broke. (Often: I'm broke)

I don't deserve it.

I'll never get there.

I want to do this, but (No excuses!)

I'll never be good enough.

It's too hard.

It's impossible.

5. WHAT DOES SUCCESS MEAN TO YOU?

Now is a great time to explore what being successful means to you. When I entered the real world after graduating from Duke University, I felt duped. I felt that life was reduced to paying bills. Everyone I knew simply went to work, paid bills, and did it over and over again with little focus on pursuing their dreams. I was certain that I wanted more than that. So, I created my very first vision board which allowed me to use my imagination to paint a picture of what I wanted my life to look like. My first vision board included pictures, words, scriptures, goals and affirmations that I knew could get me closer to the life of my dreams. I learned that we are each responsible for establishing our own barometer for what a successful life looks and feels like. My definition of success has evolved into the following:

1. I am able to leverage my gifts and talents to solve a major problem facing a target audience in an excellent way through effective business strategy.
2. I have developed the passive residual income necessary to be able to be a present wife and mom for my family.
3. I have 100% perfect health and do right by my body despite all the responsibilities that I have on my plate.
4. I am able to give back in a major way to my community.
5. I am 100% debt free.
6. I am a world traveler who is well versed on global affairs.
7. I never stop dreaming, and I am living a faith filled life.
8. I always put God first.

I encourage you to sit down and take some time to establish your definition of success and how you will know that you are successful. This might be an activity that you can do with your parents, mentors, teachers, or older siblings. Here you go!

Questions to Answer:
1. What does success mean to you?
2. How will you know when you are successful?
3. How do you want to feel when you are successful?

6. YOUR IDEAL CAREER

Now that you have established what success means to you, the time has come to start finding your ideal career. So, let us get started. Stand up, breathe in, breathe out, and repeat the following: **I BELIEVE** in myself and **I AM** ready to identify the strengths and passions I have that I can turn into a lucrative career. Anything I touch will prosper, and **I EXPECT** to enjoy what I do, do it well, and be paid very well for my expertise.

Your ideal career will be the intersection of three things: your passions, your strengths (skills), and an industry, field or problem that can pay very well. This is what I like to call your "sweet spot." Once you find your "sweet spot[4]," find opportunities that are in alignment. The careers that pay very well tend to include the things that are very hard to do and very few people know how to do them. Start brainstorming about a few of these lucrative career fields as you explore your career options. Here is a diagram that illustrates my point:

---

[4] E.g. My "sweet spot" at age 24: 1) Strengths: Mathematics, Mentoring, 2) Passions: Working with children, Education 3) Areas that Pay Very Well: Private tutoring industry

Your Goal

I am giving you one major goal. Consider it a challenge that I am personally assigning to you. I want you to hold yourself accountable to this, ok? Well here it is. Find **something you love** (your passion), that you are **very good at** (your strength), that will allow you to **earn over $100,000/year within ten years**. Yes, the goal is to earn six-figures as soon as possible. To be honest, it should not even take you ten years if you choose the correct industry and are creative about how you use your strengths (skills, gifts and talents) to add value to the world. I know a 21-year-old who is making $150,000 a year in the tech industry. I also know a 17-year-old making $30,000 a month teaching adults how to write and publish books on the kindle. Anything really is possible with the advent of technology. The focus is on a six-figure income or more. **The amount you earn will be in direct proportion to the value you provide and how the market will perceive your value.** The world is changing fast! Property values are increasing, rent is increasing, and the cost of food is increasing. It takes proper planning to stay ahead of the game, in order to live a comfortable and wonderful life. Your earning potential will dictate your quality of life.

Here is the Good News!

This wonderful career guide is filled with career opportunities that can get you to an annual income of six figures in even less time than ten years as long as you love what you do, master your craft, and take the right steps to become successful. I have carefully researched the most lucrative, rewarding careers that can make a huge difference in your future and packaged them into this book. I trust that you will carefully study these options and choose a few to explore further. Do not forget to maintain exceptional grades and obtain a top-notch SAT/ACT score to stand out among others. Secure leadership roles in your middle school and high school. Get an internship in your chosen field. Most importantly, be proactive!

Resources to Find Your Strengths and a Potential Career Path

1. www.16personalities.com
2. www.strengthstest.com
3. www.careerfitter.com
4. www.mypersonality.info

7. HOW TO BECOME MORE VALUABLE

There are only two ways to increase your value. Are you ready? Pay close attention and apply this advice so you can win in your career. These two areas are critical. It will allow you to stand out amongst your peers. When applied appropriately, you will get call backs for opportunities and people will be begging you to join their team. Ok, I will not delay any longer. You have come this far, so you totally deserve these gems. The two most important ways to increase your value is by **increasing your knowledge** and **increasing your experience** in a high-growth field. I am not referring to general, academic knowledge. I am referring to specialized knowledge about a specific industry or skill. If you love cars, study to be a well-versed mechanic, sales representative, or import and export expert. If you want to be a doctor, study everything there is to know about your area of specialty. Said differently, a sure path to success is to acquire an in-demand skill in a lucrative, fast-growing field. Oh yeah, start reading *The Economist* and stay on top of what is going on in the world so you can easily identify high-growth industries and skills that are worth acquiring. Find a mentor, study your role models and read biographies of famous individuals in your chosen field. A mentor can help you lay out a career path that is realistic and practical.

Wondering when all of this should start? I will tell you. No later than middle school. Wondering how to increase your experience? Find internships and apprenticeships fast! During your summer vacation, use that time wisely. Seek opportunities to obtain internships or shadow experts in your field of interest. Once you have done the prep work to identify the industry you would like to be in, contact someone in the field to request an informational interview. If you are under 18, bring your parent or legal guardian with you. Set up some time for you to support this person in their field and do not let them down by being late, delivering a poor work product or constantly having to be asked to perform tasks. Bring your A-game. Companies are always looking for people who are team players who can assist leaders within the organization to accomplish their mission more effectively. This is where you can come in. *Meetup.com* is a great place to find people in your chosen industry that are located in your geographical area. I would also recommend *Linkedin.com* to find professionals who are accomplished in their chosen field. Ask your parent or legal guardian to setup an account. Keep in mind; most people have a Twitter account these days, so you can always contact them directly. You just might get a response. Be bold from an early age because most of your peers will be playing video games, going to the movies, and having fun. In his book *Outliers*, Malcolm Gladwell said it will take you 10,000 hours to achieve mastery of any skill of your choice. You will have to put in the work. If you can take these extra steps to stand out and become a master at your craft, it will certainly pay off.

Always remember, value-added is the new currency. Seeking after money without finding a way to add value is a waste of your time. Keep your focus on providing something that people and organizations need. This is called a market demand. Find a way to do it faster, cheaper, and smarter.

Summary

KNOWING: <u>INCREASE YOUR KNOWLEDGE</u>
1. Maximize your educational opportunities by setting goals to obtain your college degree and an advanced degree.
2. Stay in the know about career resources and education/training opportunities.
3. Increase your knowledge about the world of work. This book is a great start!
4. Learn about the importance of gender equity and cultural diversity at school, in the work place and beyond and make it a value of yours.

DOING: <u>INCREASE YOUR EXPERIENCE</u>
5. Discover and MASTER your God-given talents, skills and abilities. Remember the 10,000 hour rule by Malcolm Gladwell.
6. Master more in-demand skills.
7. Learn how to make great decisions and negotiate your way through life!
8. Increase your work experience.

Skills Worth Mastering

A question that I am asked quite often is, "how can I determine what skills will add the most value?" This is an excellent question because we all have skills and talents to offer the world. In reality, only a small subset of those skills will allow you to be paid handsomely. This concept is best understood by studying who currently gets paid the most and evaluating why these skills bring a significant amount of value to the table.

Consider the cost of the red diamond, which is one of the most expensive, scarce and valuable gemstones[5]. It costs $1 million dollars per carat! Yes, I said that right. It is valued that high because of how rare it is. There are less than 30 red diamonds found around the entire world so you can imagine just how hard it is to find these gems. When you master the rare, hard-to-find skills, you become the gem that everyone wants to work with. Your value will require people to pay a lot of money for your expertise. Use this analogy to think about your options for skill mastery. What are skills that are very rare and very difficult to do? What are professions for which employers have a hard time finding talent? Allocate some time to grasp the "Skills Worth Mastering" list to get an idea of why certain skills can make you more marketable and be sure to generate more examples.

Consider the following questions: Who is currently paid the most and what skill or skills have they mastered? (10,000 hour rule) Why do you think this skill is valuable? Is the skill rare or common?

Skills Worth Mastering List

Skill	Rare or Common	Why is it valuable? List some characteristics
Managing Teams	Rare	
Data Science	Rare	
Public Speaking	Rare	
7-Figure Sales	Rare	
Brain Surgery	Rare	

---

[5] Schumann, Walter. "Gemstones of the World." Sterling, 2 July 2013, Print.

A few others to include are investors, entrepreneurs, specialized doctors, engineers, mathematicians, celebrities and exceptional athletes.

The most valuable people know how to do something that is _very hard_ that only a _few people_ know how to do. These people are most often paid the most. Keep this tip in mind.

What Impact Do You Want to Have on the World?

Impact, sometimes thought of as influence, is a measure of the tangible and intangible effect you have on a person, group of people, or thing. As your career develops, your goals may shift from desiring a certain level of income and personal fulfillment to developing a desire to have an impact on the world. Impact can be achieved when you find a problem that needs to be solved for a specific group of people and you provide innovative, viable solutions. The more value you bring to this specific problem, the more long-lasting and impressive your impact will be. As you think through the kind of impact you desire to have within your lifetime, use the following template as a starting point. Your impact will be most powerful, when your gifts, talents, and skills are applied toward solving a very specific problem. Remember, God made you to be the solution to someone's problem, so make it your business to allow this vision for your life to be fulfilled.

Affirmation: I am the solution to someone's problem. My gifts, talents and skills are the tools that God has given me to develop innovative, viable solutions to make the world better.

Use the following template to identify the ten biggest problems facing the world today and develop solutions for each problem. Be sure to read the newspaper, ask your parents, talk to your teachers, turn on the news and pay more attention to global politics to answer this question. People who are solution-oriented tend to be the people who advance in their career much faster than others. Use this activity to build your problem-solving muscle. You will thank me for this later.

Once you finish listing the ten biggest problems, choose one of them and commit time over the next year to bring your proposed solution to life. Complete this activity, even if your solution is simply packaged in the form of a proposal document. Then you can present your ideas to the right people who can help you to bring it to life. This will certainly impress college admissions counselors, scholarship committees and other entities who are looking for talented young people to sponsor.

What are the ten biggest problems facing the world today & what is a viable solution that can address each problem? A few examples are included. Debate with your networks.

World Problem	Your Proposed Solution
1. *E.g. Automation due to technological advances is taking away millions of jobs.*	**1.** *E.g. Generation Y and Z will have to create the jobs of tomorrow through entrepreneurial projects.*
2. *E.g. Social media and technology has caused many people to feel disconnected and depressed.*	**2.** *E.g. Develop communities and networks of people in the real world to help people to feel more connected.*
3.	**3.**
4.	**4.**
5.	**5.**
6.	**6.**

7.	7.
8.	8.
9.	9.
10.	10.

Which problem are you most interested in tackling?
Your problem of choice:

Based on your response to the previous question, provide your solution and/or plan of action to solve the selected problem.

8. COLLECT YOUR WORK IN A RESUME

Do not forget to keep track of all your amazing work and add it to your resume. If you do not know how to write a resume, I suggest you seek some guidance. I encourage you to do additional research to learn how to tailor your resume to the job and industry in which you are interested. Resume building should start in middle school and continue to grow throughout your educational career. You will find that I have included my sample resume to help you get started. In the sample, I focused on my experience related to the field of education because it is important to tailor your resume to the field for which you are applying. I secured several positions using this model. I have also provided a sample middle and high school resume. Remember, one page is the golden standard when you have less than ten years of professional experience.

Here are my ten tips for creating a winning resume:

Ten Tips for Writing a Winning Resume

1. Make sure the overall look of your resume is pleasing to the eye and the important items are easy to see within seconds. These critical items include your name, location, school name, and the companies for which you have worked. Make them bold so it pops out. Use italics for your job title/role. Use bullets to bring the reader's attention to certain points.

2. Your contact information should be at the top of your resume. Name, address, phone number, and email. Make sure you center the information and make it bold.

3. Your education should be listed at the top beginning with the most recent. Be sure to show your graduation date and most recent GPA. If necessary, you can also include your SAT scores. As you advance in your career, you will move the education section towards the end because employers will be more focused on your experience.

4. Your experiences should begin with your most recent opportunities.

5. Provide a brief sentence about what you did in the experience section for each company/organization you have worked for and specifically, highlight your impact. Do not just say what you did, but provide details on the outcome of your contribution. What did you bring to the table that no one else could have that allowed the team to experience exceptional results? What was the benefit of your work? What are your most notable accomplishments? It is always about the result.

6. As a follow up to tip number five, quantify your success in your past roles. Use a number or percent increase to measure your impact to the organization or team.
   Examples:
   - Compiled database of 1,000 potential clients to target for company expansion
   - Grew company's twitter following by 400% 100 to 500
   - Managed and developed 5 million dollars in sales pipeline with a portfolio of over 300 customers

7. Use past tense active verbs to describe your achievements, i.e., analyzed, lead, facilitated, presented, compiled, etc. You can also use present tense active verbs to describe your current roles, responsibilities and achievements, i.e., organize, execute, coordinate, oversee, administer, etc.

8. The standard headings are Education and Experience. The experience section can include both volunteer-based activities and professional commitments. Beyond that, you can include awards, skills, interests, leadership experience, volunteer experience, or any other heading that fits your professional background.

9. Cater your resume to the industry you are targeting in a clear and concise way. It is important that you choose the bullet points, activities, and past roles that will allow you to market yourself as the best person for the job. Only include the items that will make you stand out amongst the competition. If you are still in school, go ahead and include all projects, programs, internships and extracurricular activities for now, until you can acquire more relevant experience. As you advance in your career and begin to

position yourself for roles that are highly competitive, you will be able to tailor your resume accordingly.

10. Once you finish your resume, start handing it out to people. Network as often as you can to meet more people in your target industry. Find recruiters who work in your target industry and build a relationship with them. Recruiters have all the inside information, so you want them to be your best friend. Give out two resumes every week to someone who has access to opportunities. Introduce yourself using the '90-second elevator pitch[6],' and then hand them the resume. This is an excellent practice to master. The 90-second elevator pitch is a quick paragraph that you will write, rehearse, and master to be able to market yourself to anyone you meet. See chapter 12 for more information.

I AM marketable.
This means that my skills, experiences and background make me a desirable candidate.

---

[6] Source located at the end of resource guide.

TAI ABRAMS
123 Vision Boulevard Dreamville, NY 11234
(123) 456–7891
FollowYourDreams@gmail.com

EXPERIENCE

AdmissionSquad, Inc. Brooklyn, NY (NYU–Tandon) Fall 2011 – Summer 2017
Co-Founder and CEO

- Responsible for the overall leadership, growth and direction of AdmissionSquad. Developed and built high school transition program with a membership of 60 students per class year (we have serviced over 500 students to date), providing math and ELA enrichment in preparation for the high school admissions exams: Including SHSAT, ISEE, SSAT, and other HS entrance exams

- Sold test prep courses and other services to support company mission. Managed the growth and development of a robust SHSAT preparation program to bridge the gap between content taught according to the common core curriculum and content required for admissions exams

- Established strategic partnerships with middle schools, high schools, politicians and community-based organizations (non-profits and churches) to accomplish mission priorities.

- Tested over 650 6th and 7th grade scholars in NYC to grant early exposure to the SHSAT

- Key Note speaker at the 15th Lenox Academy graduation. Conducted 45+ HS workshops for parents at our home office, at local middle schools and at local events to close the information gap and get parents started earlier

- Achieved an 80% success rate consistently for three years of supporting students to gain admission into a top HS or the school of their choice. Our students have gained admission into Kent, Bronx Science, Brooklyn Latin, NEST+m, Brooklyn Tech, Bard, Packer Collegiate

- Managed a team of 5 staff and 10 volunteers to execute mission priorities across multiple business operations i.e. Business development, marketing, content development, performance tracking, budget management, scheduling, accounting, payroll and hiring

Booz Allen Hamilton, McLean, VA   Summer 2009 – Summer 2011
Consultant, Business Analytics Team

Department of Homeland Security – FEMA (April 2010 – November 2010)
Regional Coordination and Oversight: Work Stream Lead

- Facilitated and successfully executed a grants management training program delivered to ten regional offices nationwide to guide federal staff on three business processes: Award Obligations, Final Clearance Memos and Release of Funds

- Led eight professionals to develop training materials used for delivery to federal staff across ten regional offices

- Facilitated the integration of business processes and channeled all information into a final product to be delivered to government staff;

transitioned responsibilities over to ten regional offices due to contractor roll-off

Award Obligations and Notifications: Work Stream Co-Lead, Subject Matter Expert

- Efficiently managed the obligation and notification of DHS grant funds by facilitating communication between key stakeholders, building reports to quantify and monitor progress, ensuring compliance requirements have been satisfied and expeditiously notifying grant recipients of awarded grant funds in the amount of $3.4B in DHS grants (900 awards). Go-to person for client related inquiries

Risk Analysis Tool: Data Analyst

- Performed data analysis on over 1,000 line items of grant management data to design a tool in excel to identify the schedule and cost risks associated with delayed grant issuance within the grants space
- Pitched the risk analysis tool to the client using a well-messaged pitch book and successfully demonstrated the value add of implementing the tool as a mechanism to identify aging grant awards more expeditiously. Client minimized grants on hold and increased transparency around grant progression by 55%

Merrill Lynch, New York, NY   Summer 2007 & Summer 2008

Summer Analyst, Real Estate Investment Banking

- Provided thorough analysis of fixed balance sheet costs (recurring CapEx, Lease Commissions and Tenant Improvements) for Real Estate Investment Trust in preparation for IPO
- Prepared pitch book showcasing enterprise value and underperforming total returns utilizing company's over weighted debt profile, historical stock price performance and analyst market opinions

EDUCATION

Duke University, Durham, NC   Fall 2005 – Spring 2009
Bachelor of Arts in Mathematics GPA: 3.516   SAT Scores: Math 760 | Verbal 560
The American University in Cairo, Cairo, Egypt   Fall 2007
Study Abroad Arabic Language Program

ADDITIONAL INFORMATION

- **Associations:** Management Leadership for Tomorrow (MLT), Sponsors for Educational Opportunity (SEO), 4.0 schools, NAIC
- **Computer:** Microsoft Suite Proficient, HTML, Basic MatLab, QuickBooks 2011
- **Interests:** Latin Dance, Beginner Spanish, Health/Fitness, Crowd funding (Raised $10,000 and $40,000 respectively for two startups)
- **Awards:** Congressional Black Caucus Award (2005); Merrill Lynch Award for Distinction (2008); Dean's List with Distinction (Fall 2008); Caribbean Life Impact Award (2016) National Council for Negro Women Award (2017)
- **Author:** *Who Am I? An A - Z Career Guide for Teens* - A guide to help Generation Y and Z navigate the career exploration process. (June 2017)

Jehan Charles
18 West Broadway Street New York, NY 10008
(123) 456-7891
Jehan.Pitt@gmail.com

EDUCATION

The Lenox Academy, Brooklyn, NY   Fall 2013 – Spring 2016
Middle School Diploma GPA: 97.56
Regents Exams: Integrated Algebra – 95, English Language Arts – 93, Living Environment - 97

EXPERIENCE

- STEM Camp – New York, NY (1/14 – 6/16)
  - Participated in a STEM enrichment program helping to increase awareness of the STEM fields in underrepresented populations
  - Produced a science project about astrophysics and a new planet called Plant X, or Planet Nibiru exploring how close it is to Earth and the implications
- Grand Army Plaza Public Library - Brooklyn, NY (6/15 – 12/15)
  - Maintained library database for 5,000 book titles on checked-out materials
  - Sent messages to all members with past-due books
  - Coordinated volunteer math tutoring program for elementary school students (4th and 5th graders)
  - Organized card catalogue to incorporate 500 new book titles

ACTIVITIES

- Student Government President (Fall 2015 – Spring 2016)
- Spanish Club (Fall 2014 – Spring 2016)
- Cultural Enrichment Program - Ghana, West Africa (Summer 2015)
- Lacrosse Team (Fall 2013 – Spring 2015)
- Violin Lessons (5 years)

AWARDS

- Gold Honor Roll (6 quarters)
- Most Improved Student (2016)
- Outstanding Leader Award (2015)
- Community Service and Civic Engagement Award (March 2016)

REFERENCES

Available upon Request

SAMPLE HIGH SCHOOL RESUME

Candice Brown
356 Atlantic Avenue Brooklyn, NY 11201
(347) 938-4365
Candice.Brown@yahoo.com

EDUCATION

The Bronx High School of Science, Brooklyn, NY — Fall 2001 – Spring 2005
Advanced Regents Diploma GPA: 101.2 (Weighted) SAT: 1500 (M: 780, V: 720)
APs: BC Calculus, English Composition, US History, World History, Government, Chemistry, Physics, Spanish
College Courses
- **Lehman College,** Bronx, NY (*Analytic Geometry*) — Fall 2004
- **City College,** Bronx, NY (*Intro to Calculus*) — Fall 2003

EXPERIENCE

Goldman Sachs – New York, NY — Summer 2004
- Participated in an investment banking program to grant high school students an opportunity to explore I-banking and sales & trading as a career option

Girls Who Code – New York, NY — Summer 2003
- Participated in a 7-week Summer Immersion program to learn coding and get exposure to tech jobs
- Built my first mobile application to provide access to all content for the students in my math classroom at school. My app allowed students to collaborate virtually and have easy access to assignments and classroom handouts.
- Served as the student ambassador during my senior year. Recruited 10 students who were accepted into Girls Who Code for Summer 2004

National Honor Society — 2003 – present
Participated in several volunteer activities, including: building a house for Habitat for Humanity (50 hours), tutoring students to get into top NYC high schools with AdmissionSquad (80 hours), & organizing the Honor Society Induction Ceremony.

ACTIVITIES

- Student Government President (Fall 2004 – Spring 2005)
- Spanish Club (Fall 2003 – Spring 2005)
- Cultural Enrichment Program - Barcelona, Spain (Summer 2002)
- Soccer Team (Fall 2001 – Spring 2003)
- Piano Lessons (5 years)

AWARDS

Gold Honor Roll (4 quarters), Outstanding Leadership Award (2005), Most Innovative (2004), Community Service and Civic Engagement Award (April 2005)

REFERENCES

Available upon Request

9. WHAT TO DO WITH YOUR SUMMERS

The most important thing you should do with your summers is to find activities to build your resume and continue to enrich yourself through real-world opportunities. Here is a strong list of the elements you should consider while choosing what to do with your summers:

1. Engage in valuable, life-changing experiences: Advanced Placement and College Courses, Enrichment Programs, Internships, Summer Job Opportunities.

2. Acquire highly sought after skills like coding, sales, fluency in a foreign language or public speaking.

3. Expand your network with prestigious companies, firms, and organizations.

4. Meet other high performing middle and high school students across the country. This type of networking will help you to understand the competition for college admissions and will allow you to foster deeper connections with other students who are holding themselves to a standard of excellence.

5. Secure mentors in your chosen career field. Even if you switch careers, it is still good to have contacts in different industries. With the growth of technology and how quickly the world is emerging, you may get a chance to work on interdisciplinary work teams in the future. These contacts will come in handy and will add to your arsenal of expertise and experience. The goal is always to bring more to the table.

6. Make yourself more interesting. Traveling to an international country or being involved in a summer program is much better than sitting at home watching television, playing video games, or going to the mall every weekend. I know it may be tempting to relax during the summer, but summer programs & study abroad have the capacity to change your life and vastly increase your career options. Be wise about how you spend your time. You will not regret it. Note: You can still do those leisure activities, just limit it to only a few days in the summer. Feel free to do a fundraiser for your traveling goals.

10. INTERNSHIPS AND PROGRAMS FOR TEENS

In an effort to gain clarity about what you may want to do with your life, securing an internship is a great way to learn more about the field or industry you are considering. Internships are short term eight to twelve week engagements that will allow you to develop your skills and experience, while you expand your network. These opportunities, often occurring in the summer, will allow you to gain a great degree of personal growth. Lastly, it will help you to select a college major, which can be a confusing process if you have no background information on which to base your decision. Be open to traveling for an opportunity because your current city or state may not have the exact program or experience you are looking for. There are college campuses all over the world that typically host high school students for summer programs. Summer enrichment programs outside of your comfort zone can give you an advantage in the college admissions process.

Now, let us work on your pre-college professional experience. I have collected a few high-quality internships and programs that will point you in the right direction. Visit the websites listed below for more information about the application process, deadlines, admission criteria, and how these internships and programs can better prepare you for your future career. In addition, this list is **not** exhaustive. Use this list as an idea generator to find other programs of a similar calibre.

1. Youth Uprising. **Experience Gained:** Leadership and Civic Engagement www.YouthUprising.org
2. Girls Who Code. **Experience Gained:** Computer Science www.GirlsWhoCode.com
3. New York Wall Street Summer Camp for Kids and Teens. **Experience Gained:** Finance and Business Literacy, Games, Field trips to local financial districts, and Connecting with speakers from large corporations http://www.futureinvestorsclub.com/camps-newyork.cfm
4. Bank of America Student Leaders Program. **Experience Gained:** Leadership and Civic Engagement

http://about.bankofamerica.com/en-us/global-impact/student-leaders.html#fbid=pd-Lbgv77ka

5. Thurgood Marshall Summer Law Internship Program. **Experience Gained:** Exposure to Legal Professions http://www.nycbar.org/serving-the-community/diversity-and-inclusion/student-pipeline-programs/programs/thurgood-marshall-summer-law-internship

6. Summer College for High School Students at Duke University. **Experience Gained:** Earn college credit, Gain exposure to college life https://summersession.duke.edu/high-school-students/summer-college-for-high-school-students

7. Summer Academy for High School Students. **Experience Gained:** Learn how to become a global citizen, Leadership https://summersession.duke.edu/high-school-students/duke-summer-academy

8. Youth Programs at Duke University. **Experience Gained:** Varies based on Program https://learnmore.duke.edu/youth

9. Lead – Summer Business Program. **Experience Gained:** Business Principles and the skills needed for successful business careers, Increased exposure to available careers in business http://www.leadprogram.org

10. Sponsors for Educational Opportunity (SEO) Scholars Program. **Experience Gained:** Extensive support to gain admission into a top college and get a strong start to one's career http://www.seoscholars.org

11. Volunteer with your local city council leader. Check out the website and find someone who you believe in and help them! **Experience Gained:** Leadership, Civic engagement

12. NASA Interns, Fellows and Scholars. **Experience Gained:** Science Technology Engineering Mathematics (STEM), Science, Earth and Space Science exposure https://intern.nasa.gov/ossi/web/public/main/index.cfm?solarAction=view&subAction=content&contentCode=HOME_PAGE_INTERNSHIPS

13. High School program at Microsoft. **Experience Gained:** Computer Science, Programming, and STEM https://careers.microsoft.com/students/highschool

14. Computer Science Summer Institute with Google for Education. **Experience Gained:** Computer Science and Computer engineering exposure https://edu.google.com/resources/programs/computer-science-summer-institute/

15. Student Historian Program with the New York Historical Society. **Experience Gained:** Leadership, Public Speaking, and a deeper understanding of US History http://www.nyhistory.org/education/teen-programs/student-historian-program

16. High School Internships. **Experience Gained:** Varied based on opportunity www.Indeed.com

17. Management Leadership for Tomorrow (MLT) Ascend. **Experience Gained:** College Success, Career Readiness, and Increased access to college internships https://ml4t.org/mlt-ascend/

18. Expanding Horizon's Internship program with the Constitutional Rights Foundation. **Experience Gained:** Civic engagement, a deeper understanding of the Constitution and its Bill of Rights. http://www.crf-usa.org/youth-internship-program/general-information.html

19. High School Internships with the South Middlesex Opportunity Council. **Experience Gained:** Social Justice and Activism http://www.smoc.org/internship-opportunities.php

20. Student Research with Mount Sinai. **Experience Gained:** Clinical research, data entry, data collection, compile study documents, exposure to the field of medicine. http://www.mountsinai.org/locations/mount-sinai/about/volunteer/student-research

21. High School Summer Program with the Center for Excellence in Youth Education at Mount Sinai (Icahn School of Medicine). **Experience Gained:** Science enrichment, college readiness http://icahn.mssm.edu/about/diversity/ceye/programs/summer

22. Grow Your Own Business Contest. Warren Buffett's Secret Millionaires Club. **Experience Gained:** Finance and Entrepreneurship http://www.smckids.com

23. Community Board 14 Internship **Experience Gained:** Politics http://www.cb14brooklyn.com/youth/internships/

24. Volunteer with the Brooklyn Botanic Gardens. **Experience Gained:** Horticulture https://www.bbg.org/support/volunteer

25. STEM Summer Program at New York University (NYU) – Tandon School of Engineering. **Experience Gained:** STEM exposure http://engineering.nyu.edu/k12stem

Join my mailing list at TaiAbrams.com to stay up to date about more programs.

11. CAREER EXPLORATION STARTER QUESTIONS

Answer the following questions to get an idea about what your ideal career can look like.

1. What gifts and skills do I have? These are your strengths and are the things that you are extremely good at, that you can do in your sleep. Two of my gifts and skills are mathematics and public speaking.

2. What am I most passionate about? What do I love doing? I love ballroom dancing, working with the youth, inspiring and motivating people, traveling, and so much more.

3. What will the marketplace (the world) pay for? Open a newspaper or turn on the TV and pay attention to what is selling in the world today. For example, people are always getting sick, so there will always be a need for well-trained doctors and nurses. Here is another one. We live in a technology age, so people with this skillset tend to be paid very well. Finally, we have an energy problem, so solar and wind are two remedies, providing an alternate energy source. Anyone with this expertise is paid very well. Look for emerging industries and things that are hard for the common person to do. These areas tend to pay very well.

4. What are some career options that meet the first three criteria?

5. What are five emerging industries that present the biggest opportunities for innovation? Hint: Artificial Intelligence, Energy, Biotechnology all fit the description

6. What do I need to major in when I get to college?

7. Who are three people in my chosen field that I can model after and work towards meeting one day? You can email them or connect with them on Twitter. Read their book or published articles. Perform extensive research on their background. Contact them to secure an informational interview to learn about their career.

8. What are my values?

9. What type of company culture would be consistent with my values?

Homework:

1. Visit indeed.com to find a job post for the position you would like in the future. Explore the qualifications and position description. Visit glassdoor.com for salary information and reviews from past employees.

2. Study Fortune 500 companies and Fortune 100 companies to learn about the annual list of the largest companies in the United States. Fortune uses gross revenue to compile these lists. In easier terms, these lists are comprised of companies that made the most money within the last year of operation.

3. Check out Forbes.com to see the list of the most profitable industries in the world today. *The Economist* is also suitable.

I AM a lifelong learner. Learning continues beyond the classroom & even after I graduate from college.

12. 90 SECOND ELEVATOR PITCH

I always ask my students and mentees one very important question. If you were riding in the elevator with the President of the United States, what would you do? What would you say? You have exactly 90 seconds with one of the most powerful people in the world. It is important that you know what to say and how to leverage this opportunity. We call this the 90-second mini-speech or elevator pitch. An elevator pitch allows you to describe who you are and what you do, and provides an opening for a follow up or action step. You must know how to sell yourself in 90 seconds. Knowing how to sell yourself will help you to build your influence, develop trust, and drive your career success, even when you are in middle school or high school. Most people do not know how to deliver a 90 second elevator pitch. Your goal is always to stand out, so be sure to master your pitch so you can shine in any situation. You never know if one interaction with someone can turn into an opportunity.

Step One: Say hello, state your name, grade, and school you are currently attending.

Step Two: State something unique about who you are or what you do. Be creative. Think about a strength or an interest of yours.

Step Three: Use a question to initiate curiosity and healthy dialogue. The question should get the person to say yes and leave them interested in learning more about what you do.

Step Four: Keep it simple and straight to the point. Do not ramble. Get your point across in one sentence. Leave room for the person to ask you more questions. If the person asks you a question, you will know that you were effective in creating intrigue in your listener.

Step Five: End with a call to action. The call to action should include asking for their business card, asking about internship/program opportunities in a particular field or inquiring about sharing your resume. It may also include following up about supporting the person on a project in the future. For those who are in entry-level positions, the goal should always be to offer your support to the person before requesting something for yourself.

Step Six: Assuming you get the business card, be sure to follow up within 24-48 hours with a thank you email.

90 second elevator pitch example:

> Hi, my name is Tai Abrams and I am a rising senior at The Bronx High School of Science. I love math and use it to make sense of the complex world in which we live. I see mathematics as a universal language that functions as a bridge between science, business, and society. Have you noticed that most people who speak different languages can still work together by telling stories through numbers?

Let the person say, "Yes." Then continue.

> Well, I am studying how math can be used as a unifying factor on diverse data analytics teams to accomplish goals for my senior thesis paper. Can I have your card so I can share more information with you?

Let the person say, "Yes or no." Get their business card from them or find another way to stay in touch.

Follow up ASAP! If you follow these six steps, you will find it much easier to establish connections with professionals and you will go very far in your career.

13. TEN INTERVIEW QUESTIONS TO MASTER

You will participate in a variety of interviews over the span of your career, as a mechanism for a school or program to screen talent. The scholar who can answer these ten questions with finesse will shine every time. Start practicing them right now. Scholarships for college can be found as early as middle school. It is never too early to master these ten questions.

1. Tell me about yourself.
   Introduce yourself in 60-90 seconds. Demonstrate confidence, clarity, and invoke curiosity in the listener. Four to six sentences are sufficient. Your sentences should include something impressive about what you have done, e.g., I recently lead an anti-bullying initiative, mobilizing 1,000 teens to speak out against bullying at my school.

2. What do you like to do in your spare time?
   Show how cultured you are and how you use your spare time to do impressive things. It can include sports, hobbies, community service, volunteer experience, and other forms of demonstrated leadership.

3. What motivates you and why?
   Talk about what drives you. What is your why? Why do you push yourself to do well in school and get involved in activities? Think about a solid answer for this question that shares more about your character.

4. What impact do you want to have on the world?
   Answering this question successfully will show the interviewer your ability to think big. You can show how aware and savvy you are with the happenings in the world. Talk about a big problem facing the world today and how you plan to solve it. An excellent activity is to sit down one day and write down what you think the ten biggest problems are that the world is facing today (See chapter 7 for more details). I will give you a hint for the first one: climate change. Look it up! Once you have written them down, start exploring solutions to these ten problems. If you fall in love with one of them, I challenge you to take your solution to the next level by starting a research project around it to begin to implement the idea. This additional research will make you stand out. See the activity sheet in chapter 7 to help you structure your answer.

5. If you could change one thing about your school or program, what would it be and why? Provide a plan of action to address the growth opportunity.
Demonstrate your ability to be a problem solver, solution-oriented, and highly innovative.

6. Why are you interested in this school or company?
Show that you did your research and that you understand why the school, program, or company is a good fit for who you are and where you are on your career or academic journey.

7. Where do you see yourself in five years?
Share the vision you have for your life. Most people lack vision. To be able to articulate a five-year plan is to be able to demonstrate maturity, planning, and a goal-oriented mindset.

8. Tell me about a strength of yours.
Talk about what you are good at, and of that, what you are most proud of.

9. Tell me about a weakness of yours.
Talk about an opportunity for growth that you have been proactive about correcting. It should be a strength in disguise or at least demonstrate strength through the power of self-reflection.

10. Tell me about a time when you overcame adversity.
Show how resilient you are and what you do when life gets tough.

14. THE LISTS YOU NEED TO KNOW ABOUT

The next few pages contains the lists you need to know about. I have included the five teens you need to know, the 30 college majors that lead to unemployment or low pay, 18 high-paying careers, 25 skills to master to make you more valuable, the ten most valuable college majors, and the 15 people you need to study to learn to build wealth. There are teens out there who are doing phenomenal things with their time before heading to college. You would be impressed to know that there are teenagers who have already figured out how to generate six-figures before they even turn 18. These teens should be the ones to which you pay close attention. I have also included the skills that are most valuable in present day society that you could benefit from learning and mastering.

While unemployment is always present, you would be surprised to know that there are a plethora of jobs that exist that need talent. The challenge is that there are not enough people with the skills needed to fill those positions. If you could be one of the few people out there with these skills, it would set you apart from other young professionals that you are competing with and your stock would go up. This means that you would be worth more to a company and they would have to compensate you accordingly. Your path toward financial prosperity lays right here in this resource guide. All you need to do is take the information and apply it. Become a master at something that will make you valuable. I have said this multiple times, so you should know that I am very serious. The more skills you have, the more valuable you become. Get to learning and mastering.

The 6-7 Figure Crew
Meet Five Model Teens Who Learned How to Earn BIG!

This list includes five teens who made over six-figures during their teenage years. Yup! Before they turned 18, they figured out how to earn over $100,000. If they can do it, so can you! The only difference between these teens and you is that they decided to use their free time as a teen, tween, or even younger, to literally change the world. They are innovators, entrepreneurs, and self-starters using their passions to build a career that adds value and is quite lucrative at the same time. Take notes!

1. Temper Thompson[7]: While most teens were playing video games, going to the movies, asking their parents for money, or working minimum wage jobs, Temper Thompson was getting busy figuring out how to earn money for himself. He started in 8th grade and spent his free time exploring the very lucrative world of internet marketing. By age 17, he was making $30,000 a month selling courses on how to publish books on Kindle. The Inc.com's article "How the 17-year-old genius is making more than $30,000 each month on the internet," we get to meet the young, savvy Temper Thompson who shared with us his five tips about how to position yourself to earn that kind of dough. You can totally do it too! The author Joel Comm asks the very important question, "What's your excuse?" He is totally right. We all have the same access that Temper did. Temper applied himself, got creative, and found a way to show up for his target audience. Check him out at temperthompson.com.

   Here are his five tips:
   a. Take action
   b. Don't fear failure
   c. Stay focused
   d. Surround yourself with positive people
   e. Don't get comfortable

2. Gabriel Jordan: This rock star teen started her jewelry business when she was only nine years old and has already figured out how to generate six-figures in revenue annually! She is the author of *The Making of a Young Entrepreneur* and the CEO of Excel Youth Mentoring Institute. Can I also add, that she is a speaker and has won over 20 awards? She said, "When I reflect back on my life, I want it to be filled with big dreams, big actions, and big accomplishments, and that's what I want for others." Well, all I have to say is Miss Gabriel Jordan is living up to her dreams. Visit her website at www.gabriellejordaninspires.com.

---

[7] Source located at the end of resource guide.

3. Evan TubeHD[8]: Nine-year old Evan and his father Jared, started a YouTube channel about one of their biggest passions, toys. They started the channel to have the opportunity to bond with one another. Soon enough, the channel attracted thousands of viewers. Thousands quickly grew to millions and the rest in history. To date, the channel has brought in over a billion views allowing this family to generate about $1.3 million annually from advertisement sales. With his extreme popularity, Evan is also invited to participate in other lucrative projects.

Evan's father, Jared, has five tips for you:
   a. Be persistent
   b. Know your audience
   c. Embrace your inner youth
   d. Provide value to your viewer
   e. Be unique

4. Ashley Qualls[9]: At age 14, Ashley Qualls was already earning $70,000 per month and had seven million monthly visitors, which makes her a teenage millionaire. Yes, you read that correctly. What most people strive to earn in one year, she was earning in one month. Her business of choice? Online design. She launched WhateverLife.com to provide graphic design and website layout services to Myspace users. Want to know what her life is like? Here are a few words from Ashley, "It's a busier schedule. There's more to keep track of, whether its finance or employees and making sure everything is up to date and the content is secure." She started this business with $80 that she borrowed from her mom and found success using the most basic principle of capitalism, the law of supply and demand. Ashley's million-dollar business has given her and her working-class family a sense of financial security they had never really known and she did this by finding a growing trend—online social networking—and provided a product to fill the desires of the market. Remarkable story.

[8] Grothaus, Michael. "Meet the Father-Son Team Making $1.3 Million on YouTube." Fast Company, Inc. Mansueto Ventures, LLC., 4 May 2015, Web. 15 Apr 2017.

[9] Salter, Chuck. "Girl Power." Fast Company, Inc. Mansueto Ventures, LLC., 1 Sep 2007, Web. 15 Mar 2017.

Here is what I learned from Ashley's story that I want to share with you:

    a.   You need a strong work ethic to accomplish goals this big.

    b.   You need to stay very focused, even when everyone around you is having fun.

    c.   Your peer group can be your target market. Figure out what they may need.

    d.   Find a mentor and hire experts when necessary. It takes money to make money.

    e.   Have confidence and believe in your vision.

5.   Mark Bao: This phenomenal teen was the founding partner of 11 technology startups and had three foundations by age 17. At age 16, he sold his first company. In fifth grade, he used Visual Basic 6.0 to write a simple computer application that helped him write his school essays and managed his homework. Once finished, he copied the program onto floppy discs and sold them to his friends. Basically, he created a winning product. In response to the question, "What do you want to be when you grow up?" Here is his answer, "I still want to do entrepreneurship. Avecora, the company I am most proud of, is helping people communicate better and experience technology in a new way. That's the company that I want to build an empire out of. We're always working on the non-profits as well. My preliminary life goal right now is to donate 80% to humanitarian aid and research. Since my life goal for my career is to earn $10 billion, that would be $8 billion. Another 10% will go to The Mark Bao Foundation, where we manage research grants and lobby for better funding for NASA and the National Institute of Health (NIH). Another 5% will go to funding start-ups, helping them grow."

    So, there you have it. Five extraordinary teens. I hope this gives you more clarity about why I am pushing you to do more earlier. Think bigger, dream bigger, and work your butt off to become exceptional. These teens are far ahead of the average teen because they have mastered many career principles during their teenage years; they will be successful for the rest of their life. I am not even talking six-figures, or even seven-figures. These teens are on track for billion-dollar success. Mark Zuckerberg, the founder of Facebook, started coding when he was in middle school and built an online text-messaging program for his dad's company before he turned 13. If there are any secrets I could share with you, it is that the vision for your career must start earlier and that you must master a skill that will allow you to build or create products that sell. Now, get to work!

I would like to leave you with a challenge. Think long and hard about a problem that needs to be solved that is a major pain point for people. Perform extensive research to find out how to show up for this audience. This group will be called your target market. A target market is a particular group of customers at which a product or service is aimed[10]. Once you have the right idea that will address their most pressing problem, monetize it. Start marketing and selling your product or service so it can improve the lives of your customers. Submit your success story to **info@TaiAbrams.com** for a chance to be featured.

---

[10] Friedman, Jack P. *Dictionary of Business and Economic Terms*. Dallas: Barron's Educational Services, 2012. Print.

Eighteen High-paying Careers[11]

Learn about eighteen careers that can lead to you earning the big bucks. These career options are lucrative and require you to develop skills that most people are not willing to master. While time is on your side, learn more about these career paths and master the skills so you can make it to the top.

	Career	Median Salary/ Revenue	Industry
1	Investor	Billionaire Potential	Any
2	CEO	$13,800,000	Any
3	Entrepreneur	Billionaire Potential	Any
4	C-Suite Positions	$278,800	Any
5	Investment Banker	$250K-$20M (w/ bonus)	Finance
6	Anesthesiologist	$258,100	Healthcare
7	Surgeon	$247,520	Healthcare
8	Obstetrician & Gynecologist	$222,400	Healthcare
9	Physician	$197,700	Healthcare
10	Nurse Anesthetist (CRNA)	$170,000	Healthcare
11	Lawyer	$144,500	Law
12	Research & Development Manager	$142,120	Any
13	Software Development Manager/Devops Engineer	$132,000	Tech
14	Pharmacy Manager	$130,000	Healthcare
15	Strategy Manager	$130,000	Business
16	Software Architect	$128,250	Tech
17	Integrated Circuit Designer Engineer	$127,500	Tech
18	Data Scientist	$109,399	Tech

[11] Source located at the end of the resource guide.

Do You Want to Be Really, Really Rich?

Some of you may have a deep, burning desire to become very wealthy during your time here on this Earth and I want to make sure that you understand exactly what it will take to get there. If you can recall the Skills Worth Mastering list, you can understand that the people who are paid the most in society are the folks who provide the most value. These are the folks who have mastered something that is very hard to do that few people know how to do. To get to exceptional levels of wealth it gets even more specific than that. Out of all the strategies, tools, industries, skills and ideas that you may have and/or know about, you must travel down one narrow, difficult, highly-rewarding path to get to extreme levels of wealth. Are you ready? Here's the answer. You must become an entrepreneur. Get a pen and paper to write this one down and say it out loud.

In order to become really rich, I need to own a business, or businesses, that becomes so valuable I can sell it. I can choose whether or not I want to sell, but it is important that I have the option based on the quality of what I have built. I must become an entrepreneur and master sales to make this happen.

I want you to say this to yourself to make it clear to yourself what it really takes. The pathway of entrepreneurship requires long hours with a huge investment of time, energy, capital (money) and a whole lot of risk. If you end up building a successful company, you will be amongst the wealthiest people in the entire world. When you invest in yourself, take a risk and build a team that you invest in as well, these opportunities will become possible to you. You must solve the right problem for the right audience so you can build something with massive staying power. Keep in mind, Bill Gates worked 16 hour days throughout all of his 20's to build Microsoft. He sacrificed his younger years to create a life of prosperity. He also knew how to sell. The wealthiest people in the world know how to sell anything from a coconut to an artificial intelligence system. They also know how to sell themselves and get people to invest in their vision of the future. If you do not want to be a billionaire, you can still be a millionaire. If you can sell 1 million units (silly bandz, fidget spinners, slime, etc.) at a dollar, you are a millionaire. Your consistency and discipline in selling will allow you to accomplish this goal. The following chart includes 15 people to study to learn more about this career option.

Fifteen People to Study to Learn How to Build Wealth[12]
The Self-Made Billionaires[13]

	Name	Company/Source of Wealth	Net Worth
1	Bill Gates	Microsoft	$85.7 billion
2	Warren Buffet	Berkshire Hathaway	$70.1 billion
3	Amancio Ortega	Zara	$65 billion
4	Larry Ellison	Oracle	$51.5 billion
5	Mark Zuckerberg	Facebook	$46.8 billion
6	Jeff Bezos	Amazon	$39.8 billion
7	Carlos Slim	Telecom	$35.4 billion
8	Sam Walton	Walmart	$34.9 billion
9	Larry Page	Google	$29.7 billion
10	Jack Ma	Alibaba	$22.7 billion
11	Aliko Dangote (Nigeria)	Dangote Cement (Also sugar & flour)	$12.1 billion
12	Mike Adenuga (Nigeria)	Telecom, oil	$5.8 billion
13	Robert F. Smith	Vista Equity Partners	$3.7 billion
14	Oprah	Oprah Winfrey Network (OWN)/, Harpo Studios	$3.1 billion
15	Folorunsho Alakija (Nigeria)	Famfa Oil	$1.6 billion

Honorable Mention
- Research the story of Reginald Lewis. He performed almost a billion-dollar leveraged buyout in the late 1980's. It was the first international leveraged buyout of its kind.
- Check out Alphabet, Inc.

Note: For those who do not become an entrepreneur, you still need to focus on ownership and growing your investments. I will say it again; career success and financial success go together. Make it a priority!

[12] Peterson-Withorn, Chase. "Forbes Billionaires: Full List Of The 500 Richest People In The World 2015." Forbes.com. Forbes Media, LLC., 02 Mar 2015, Web. 16 Apr 2017.

[13] Martin, Emmie and Danner, Christi. "The 25 Richest Self-made Billionaires." BusinessInsider.com. Axel Springer SE, 16 June 2015, Web. 10 Feb 2017.

Thirty College Majors that Pay the Least

Your college major is a part of your career path. It is the first formal opportunity you have, to get training and information about your chosen field and even build skills. I have noticed many teens make a misinformed decision about their major. I have decided to include the majors for which you need to avoid incurring massive debt and the majors that are the most valuable. Remember, college is supposed to be an investment. Treating college as an investment would mean that the time, money and energy spent during your four years in college should allow you to graduate being worth more than you were, before you began. Currently, the minimum wage rate is $15.00 per hour. This is the amount of money you are worth before going to college. If you graduate being paid, the same or even less, you wasted your time. In this case, your college experience was a bad investment.

I have provided you with the least valuable college majors that you need to avoid when you go to college. Remember, you can always purchase extra books and attend courses outside of school, if you have a deep interest in a topic that is on this list. You want to make sure that your time and monetary investment is placed into a degree program that will make you worth more to the marketplace. The goal is always to increase your value.

This list is based on very high initial unemployment rates, on average 10%, and low initial earnings[14]. This means that it is highly likely that you will graduate without a job or you will be paid very little money. It is highly likely that you will only be able to secure a job paying minimum wage. This leads to the question of whether your time in college was worth it. College is always worth it as long as you spend your time learning and building skills that will make your time worthwhile. If you have an interest in one of these careers and would like to explore it as a supplement to your career options, consider it as a minor in college or pursue it on a self-study basis. There are also certificate programs and trade schools that are a healthy alternative.

---

[14] "The Least Valuable College Majors." *Georgetown University Center on Education and the Workforce (CEW)*. Forbes Media, LLC., 2009 and 2010 American Community Survey, Web. 16 Apr 2017.

Here they are: Majors are listed in no particular order.

	College Major	Median Earnings for Recent Graduates	Median Earnings for Experienced Graduates
1	Psychology & Sociology	$35,100	$54,600
2	History	$32,000	$54,000
3	Social Work	$33,200	$45,700
4	Counseling	$32,300	$40,900
5	Philosophy, Theology, Religious/Bible Studies	$30,000	$48,000
6	Liberal Arts	$30,000	$50,000
7	Music	$30,000	$45,000
8	Physical Fitness & Parks Recreation	$30,000	$50,000
9	Commercial Art & Graphic Design	$32,000	$49,000
10	English Language & Literature	$32,000	$52,000
11	Film, Video & Photographic Arts	$30,000	$50,000
12	Special Education	$35,500	$47,800
13	Horticulture	$35,400	$49,400
14	Culinary Arts & Food Service Management	$35,400	$53,000
15	Music Teacher Education	$34,300	$53,100
16	Exercise Science	$35,200	$56,000
17	Anthropology & Archeology	$28,000	$47,000
18	Therapeutic Recreation	$33,800	$48,00
19	Secondary English Teacher Education	$35,000	$63,400
20	Fine Arts	$30,000	$45,000
21	Early Childhood/Art/ Elementary Education	$32,900	$42,300
22	Child & Family Studies	$30,900	$39,600
23	Youth Ministry	$32,200	$45,400
24	Human Services	$34,100	$43,400

25	Health Administration	$34,600	$56,100
26	Animal Science	$34,700	$57,000
27	Human Development & Family Studies	$34,700	$48,500
28	Broadcast Communication	$34,800	$66,200
29	Graphic Design, Illustration	$35,700	$61,800
30	Family and Consumer Science	$35,800	$54,000

Ten College Majors that Yield the Highest Return on Investment (ROI)

As an alternative, there are several majors, that can lead to high-paying jobs, that will yield a substantial **Return on Investment** (ROI). In the long run, you will get more out than what you initially invested. These majors will allow you to reap the rewards of a college degree.

Here they are: Majors are listed in no particular order.

	College Major	Median Earnings for Recent Graduates	Median Earnings for Experienced Graduates
1	Engineering (software engineering if available)	$65,000 - $101,000	$115,000 - $168,000
2	Computer Science	$62,900	$107,000
3	Physics	$55,500	$106,000
4	Applied Mathematics	$55,800	$102,000
5	Economics	$52,100	$98,500
6	Management Information Systems	$56,800	$96,300
7	Finance	$51,900	$89,100
8	Government and Political Science	$42,600	$88,200
9	Construction Project Management	$50,700	$83,300
10	Biochemistry and Molecular Biology	$44,100	$91,400

Be sure to get 2-3 internships on your resume while you are in college before you start applying for a full-time position post-graduation. Internships will give you a chance to get a feel for your professional industry, while also allowing you to learn some skills that will set you apart during the recruitment process.

Best Advanced Degree Programs
Listed in no particular order[15]

An advanced degree is an excellent way to learn more about your chosen industry and become an expert in your field. People typically go back to school after gaining a few years of experience in their career to pursue a Master's degree or a Doctor of Philosophy (Phd). Advanced degrees can be used to go deeper in your career or to change directions if you would like to try out a new career path. A Doctor of Philosophy should be considered if you have a deep interest in research and teaching in colleges/universities across the nation. A salary increase is a very common benefit to completing a Master's degree or higher. Here are a few advanced degree programs to consider a few years after you graduate from college:

1. Master's in Business Administration (MBA)	10. Management Information Systems
2. Computer Science (Computer and Information Systems)	11. Applied Mathematics/ Analytics (Big Data)
3. Pharmacy, Pharmacology	12. Software Engineering
4. Economics	13. Physical Chemistry
5. Finance	14. Physics
6. Biostatistics or Statistics	15. Physician's Assistant
7. Political Science	16. Law School
8. Nurse Anesthetist	17. Medical School
9. Engineering (Various types))	18. Organic Chemistry

[15] Dishman, Lydia. "Best and Worst Graduate Degrees for Jobs in 2016." *Fortune.com.* Time Inc., 21 Mar 2016, Web. 16 Apr 2017.

Twenty-five Most Valuable Skills to Master[16]

The formula is simple. The more valuable skills you have in your arsenal → the more valuable you become → the more money you earn. Here are the twenty-five most valuable, in-demand skills that will make you stand out in the 21st century. Choose one that you love and start mastering it early!

1. INVESTING

Learn how to identify appropriate investments that can yield a high return. **Foundational K-12 Skill: Mathematics**

2. BIG DATA

Making Sense of Big Data: With increased information about customers and the world around us, employers need people who know how to organize, analyze data, apply, and arrive at great conclusions. Primary Skills: Data Mining, Data Warehousing, Data Modeling, Statistical Analysis System (SAS), Customer Service Metrics. **Foundational K-12 Skill: Mathematics, Statistics, Coding**

3. BUSINESS

Managing the Bottom Line: Knowing what keeps a company profitable (a company is profitable when it produces positive earnings after all expenses are deducted) will make you a more valuable member of the team. Understand how day-to-day deals and decisions affect profitability. Primary Skills: Financial Accounting, Profit and loss statement, Contract Negotiation, Financial Analysis, Forecasting, New Business Development. **Foundational K-12 Skill: Mathematics, Economics**

4. TECHNOLGY

Wrangling New Tech Primary Skills: Software Development, Search Engine Marketing, Customer Service Metrics, Systems, Applications, Products in Data Processing (SAP) Material Management, Information Technology (IT) Security and Infrastructure, Computer-Aided Design/Manufacturing. **Foundational K-12 Skill: Mathematics, Intro to Computer Science**

---

[16] Source located at the end of resource guide.

5. STRATEGY

Workers who are adept at identifying business needs and valuable solutions by thinking strategically tend to earn more. Primary Skills: Strategic Planning, Business Analysis, Strategic Project Management. Foundational K-12 Skill: Mathematics, Economics, Game: Chess

6. SALES

Every company, big or small, needs people to sell their products and services to customers. The person who has the highest sales volume is one of the most valuable members of a team. Primary Skills: Technical Sales. Foundational K-12 Skill: Public Speaking/Story Telling, Psychology, Works well with people and excellent communication, Mathematics

7. OPERATIONS

Companies need people who know how to assess and minimize operational threats (risk) and this applies to a wide array of industries. Primary Skills: Risk Management/Risk Control, Lean Manufacturing, Systems Troubleshooting. Foundational K-12 Skill: Mathematics, Strong General Education

8. HEALTHCARE

There is always a need for doctors, nurses, and healers at large so there will always be a need for people to educate and train them. Primary Skills: Clinical Education. Foundational K-12 Skill: Strong General Education

15. THE POWER OF AN ALUMNI NETWORK

Have you ever heard of the saying, "You are the average of the five people you hang around?" Well, if not, let me be the first person to tell you that it is very true. I would get so annoyed when my mom would constantly say, "Birds of a feather flock together," as a reminder to be mindful of the people I was hanging around in high school. I was so sure that I was an independent thinker that could not be swayed or manipulated. What I did not realize is that even when my friends were not intentionally influencing me, I was still picking up many of their habits—both the good and the bad. My mom was right and once I realized this, I got much more intentional about who I would hang around as I navigated my career journey and moved towards being successful.

Once I became more thoughtful about the type of people I wanted to be around, I started to find the folks who could help me to reach my goals more expeditiously. I used something called an alumni network to hasten this process. An alumni network is a collection of people that you have perpetual access to because you have a shared experience of matriculating through a school, college, program, or group together. For example, since I attended the Bronx High School of Science, Duke University, and participated in MLT, I now have access to their alumni networks, full of talented people that are ahead of me in the career process. I get to meet CEO's, executives, entrepreneurs, investment bankers, lawyers, partners and doctors on a regular basis because of the schools I attended and programs for which I was a member. These people are only a phone call, an email, or an introduction away. Make sure you are finding schools, programs, and groups that have the kind of alumni network with which you want to be associated. From these networks, I found mentors, "growth friends," and accountability partners and this pushed me toward the career and life of my dreams. Do everything in your power to get into a top high school, a top college and a top program for your advanced degree. Remember, the fastest way to build a successful career is to talk to people who are playing the game at a higher level than you are. Elite schools and programs tend to have exclusive networks filled with these types of people and this kind of access will make your career journey much easier.

These people will be the folks that you can call on when you need advice or are in need of an opportunity. Your first mentor may be found in these circles. I have another saying for you, "Your network is your net worth." If you want to make sure you earn more, you are going to need to know people who earn more. Being connected to wealthy people will push you to become an impactful, successful, and wealthy person. Find these folks and hold onto them. Reach into your school's database to find people who have studied the majors you are interested in or are currently in careers in which you are interested. Go ahead and connect with them. Build and maintain these relationships, so they can be an asset to you as you figure out what you really want to do with your career. Your alumni network will serve as a strong support system as you advance in your chosen field. Who they know is who you know because they can simply introduce you to the person. This is where the whole concept of the six degrees of separation came from. You are only six degrees away from the president of the United States. You know someone, who knows someone, who knows someone, who can get you to the president of the United States. It is really that simple. Once you master the networking game, you will maximize your career opportunities.

Always remember, the connections that you form and cultivate are assets. Leverage your connections to catapult your career.

Here are a few best practices to cultivate your network and secure your dream mentors:

1. Make a list of the people you already know who have knowledge or experience in your job/field of interest.

2. Contact your alumni association and other community & professional organizations for which you are a member.

3. Connect with people in-person not just online or through social media.

4. Find a mentor and other advocates. Follow them and engage with them on social media. These are the people you can learn from, who will be your biggest cheerleaders.

5. Meet with your mentor 2-4 times a year, preferably in-person, but a phone call is also acceptable.

6. Add value first! Bring something to the table that will make the other person's life easier. Mutually beneficial relationships are always better. Offer to help with a research project or pursue an apprenticeship.

7. Send an update email to all your supporters at least once a year with an update about how you are doing. Be sure to blind carbon copy (bcc) everyone on the email. E.g. Teachers, mentors, friends, colleagues, co-workers, aunts, uncles, etc.

8. Send a thank you note after in-person interviews and send congratulatory notes to highlight the career achievements of others.

16. YOUR CAREER GUIDE FROM A - Z

Now that we have covered all the preliminary work that you will need to do to position yourself for career success, I think you are ready for your A to Z career guide[17]. Here is a list of awesome careers from A to Z to get you started on the career exploration process. If you are reading this, I know you will be successful because it means that you are being proactive about finding your ideal career. At its core, success is when preparation meets opportunity. You will need to prepare for the day when your major opportunity crosses your path. A goal without a well-thought-out plan cannot be carried out efficiently and effectively. You should want to take your dreams, break them down into tangible goals, and proceed with a highly structured, thorough plan. By completing the activities included in this guide and exploring the career path that interests you most, you will already be ahead of the game. I speak success, joy, fulfillment, and perfect self-expression into your life, and I encourage you to do this thought work earlier rather than later so you can get a strong start to your career. When you have a clear vision for your life and develop a plan to get there, you can move forward with a great deal of confidence knowing that you have a roadmap to guide you toward your destination. It is okay if the plan changes. It is not okay to wander this earth filled with limitless opportunity without a plan at all. Your chance to create an extraordinary life filled with purpose begins right now. So, let us get started!

I wish you all the best!

Salary Classification Key: Based on Income Potential	
Bronze	$50,000 - $99,999
Silver	$100,000 - $199,999
Gold	$200,000 - $299,999
Platinum	$300,000 - $999,999
Titanium	$1,000,000+

---

[17] Salary classification is based on income potential. Visit the Bureau of Labor Statistics for more information. https://www.bls.gov/ooh/home.htm Salary data is not available for all careers and may adjust from year to year. Do the necessary research to find the most up to date number and to familiarize yourself with your chosen industry.

Air

> **Airline Pilot:** I AM responsible for flying aircraft for airlines that transport people and cargo from place to place, on a fixed schedule. I have a very important job of making sure everyone gets to his or her destination safely. I have earned a Private Pilot certificate. I have also earned an instrument rating and a multi-engine rating. I attended an aviation program approved by the Federal Aviation Administration (FAA). I have my Commercial Pilot certificate. I have at least 1800 hours of flight experience for my licensure. I have a good credit score. A four-year bachelor's degree is preferred. Also known as Aviator. Salary: Silver.

> **Air Traffic Controller:** I AM in love with all things that happen in the air and I help to maintain the flow of air traffic in a safe, orderly, and expeditious way. The same way we can be stuck in traffic when driving in cars, this can happen in the sky as well. I make sure there are no collisions in the air. I have a 4-year degree in air traffic control. I have a certification from the Federal Aviation Authority (FAA), from the military, or from a Collegiate Training Initiative (CTI) school. Salary: Silver.

> **Copilot:** I AM second in command to fly the aircraft and I control certain portions of the functions needed to fly the plane effectively. I plan to be promoted to Pilot in Command (PIC) very soon. Identical degree, experience, and certifications as a pilot (see above). Salary: Silver.

> **Air/Flight Engineers:** I ensure that all parts of the plane are in proper working order before it is cleared and ready to go for takeoff. I have a very thorough checklist that I use to complete this inspection. I am responsible for any repairs needed if a mechanical issue does arise. I have a bachelor's

degree in aeronautical or mechanical engineering. Salary: Silver.

> **Flying Car Designer:** I design flying cars that will be used in the future. I build cars for ground transportation too. I have a degree in industrial design, mechanical engineering, or electrical engineering. Salary: Bronze.

Agriculture
> **Agribusiness Management:** I own or manage farms and ranches. I can also work for separate businesses that exist to support farms and ranches. I have a Bachelor of Science and Master's in agribusiness. Salary: Silver.

> **Farmer (Organic Farmer):** I grow and supply the food needed to feed people all over the world. I make sure that the animals, foods, and plants are grown in a safe and sustainable way. I AM concerned about Genetically Modified Organisms (GMO) that are being put into the foods. I work hard to bring high quality food to people. I have a bachelor's degree in agricultural economics and agricultural business management. My studies included information about agriculture, farm management, dairy science, animal science, and the conservation of natural resources. Salary: Bronze.

> **Food Scientist:** I improve food products and create new products by researching and experimenting with combinations of raw ingredients, food sources, and food processing techniques. For example, Louis Pasteur discovered the food processing method named after him. Food scientists developed the thin, individually wrapped, square slices of pasteurized cheddar and Swiss cheese that never go bad. Salary: Bronze.

> **Truck Driving Company Owner/Operator:** I have drivers that help to ship large quantities of meat, fruits, and vegetables vast distances without spoilage. No education

requirements. Purchase truck and secure a commercial driver's license. Salary: Silver.

➤ **Food Packaging Manager:** I manage a team of people who package agricultural products safely and appropriately for shipment. I also have packing operational equipment and employ my skills and experience to operate them. My industry thrives in places like California, Texas, and portions of the Midwest and South because agriculture is a huge part of their economy. I have a degree in operations management and supervision. Salary: Bronze.

➤ **Other:** Agricultural and Natural Resources Communications, Horticulturist, Auditing Clerks. Research these careers for more details.

Athlete (See Sports): I have a dream to go to the Olympics and win a medal. Income will vary based on sport and is mostly based on sponsorships and endorsements once you win a medal or land a spot on the starting team. This is a risky career path. One injury and your career is over and it is very competitive. Other careers provide you with long-term income security. The lifetime earning potential of a sports player is lower than the lifetime earning potential of a software engineer. You can become wealthy using your brain[18].

➤ **Basketball Player (National Basketball Association - NBA):** I play on a team of five with a goal to get the most number of basketballs into the basket. Salary: Titanium.

➤ **Fencer:** I use a sword to compete against my opponent.

➤ **Football Player (National Football League - NFL):** Salary: Titanium but the career path is very short lived. Football players usually last for about 5 years (age 22-27) and significant damage is done to their brain due to severe collisions.

---

[18] Source located at the end of resource guide.

➢ **Runner:** I run both long distances and short distances and hop over things.

➢ **Soccer Player (Major League Soccer - MLS):** My primary objective is to get the ball into the goal. I can use everything on my body except for my hands. Salary: Titanium.

➢ **And so many more:** Hockey (National Hockey League - NHL), Baseball (Major League Baseball - MLB), Lacrosse, Gymnastics, Swimming, and more. There are so many wonderful sports. Find one you will love if you have the gift of being an athlete.

Architecture

➢ **Architect:** I AM an architect and I design buildings and huge structures. My work is known all over the world. I have a bachelor's degree in architecture. Salary: Bronze.

➢ **Architectural Engineer/Structural Designer:** I AM trained to calculate, understand, and predict the strength, rigidity, and stability of development projects, including both building and non-building structures. I also supervise a team of construction workers on the development site. The Eiffel Tower was one of the victories of a team of structural engineers working together to achieve a successful end product. I have a degree in civil engineering. Salary: Bronze.

Art

➢ **Artistic (Art) Director:** I AM responsible for supervising and unifying the vision of the project I am directing. I AM specifically responsible for the visual style and images in the projects I oversee and direct a team of artists to deliver the final work product. I can work in a variety of sectors, including theater, advertising, magazines, newspapers, film, video games, marketing, internet, publishing and fashion. I work mostly in New York. I have a bachelor's degree in art or design. Salary of top 10%: Silver.

➤ **Art Gallery Owner:** I AM responsible for running the entire operation of my art gallery. I AM a community advocate and seller of art and I spend my workday intimately involved in all aspects of this venture, including the art itself, office duties, creating events, and publishing professional materials to spotlight the gallery. I also manage a team of curators and assistants to ensure that things run smoothly. I have a bachelor's degree in art management. Salary: Silver.

➤ **Curator:** I AM a content specialist and the primary keeper or custodian of all the art pieces in a gallery. I get to play the important role of selecting the pieces to include within the art gallery. The word curator means, "to take care" in Latin. I have a bachelor's and master's degree in art, history, archeology, museum studies, or a related field. Salary: Bronze.

Additional Options: Anthropologist, Archaeologist, Artist, Astronomer.

Bankers: The following professions deal with money. To succeed in any of the following professions you will need a degree in finance, economics, business, accounting, mathematics, or a related field while in college. Make sure you secure an internship at a top bank during the summer after your junior year. If you can secure one even earlier, DO IT!

➤ **Asset Manager/Private Wealth Manager:** I manage the money and investments of individuals, families, and companies. Money and investments that a person or company owns are called assets and need to be managed so it can continue to grow. I create an organized way of maintaining, increasing, and disposing of assets in the most cost-effective manner possible. Salary: Silver.

> **Investment Banker:** I work in a financial institution that is in the business primarily of raising capital (money) for companies, governments, and other entities. If a company wants to purchase another company, they come to me. If a company wants to use debt to buy a company, they come to me. If a company wants to by a real estate investment trust, they come to me. I work on teams to facilitate these transactions. My work is conducted in a large bank's division that is involved with these activities, often called an investment bank. The bulge bracket firms get to work on the biggest transactions in the world today! Goldman Sachs, Morgan Stanley, and Credit Suisse are three of them. Salary: Platinum

> **Finance Manager:** I make sure my company's financials are doing great! I produce financial reports, direct investment activities, and develop strategies and plans for the long-term financial goals of the company. Salary: Silver.

> **Private Equity:** I am an analyst supporting my firm to decide which investments make the most sense. I help large companies, institutions, and accredited investors take their money and invest in companies that do not trade on the stock market. My company charges a 2% management fee and 20% of all profits gained from the sale of a company. My firm has about $1 billion in assets under management (AUM). Salary: Silver Entry Level.
>
> **Q:** What is an Accredited Investor?
> **A:** Someone who makes $200,000 a year or $300,000 with a spouse for the last two years OR someone with a net worth exceeding $1 million, individually or with a spouse.

> **Equity Research Associate:** I perform research on today's most attractive companies with an objective of making a stock investment recommendation to BUY, SELL, or HOLD. I also analyze a company's financials, perform ratio analysis, and forecast the financials (financial

modeling). All my work is communicated in something called an **equity research** report and thousands of people rely on my insight to make decisions on what to do with their money. I cover a small group of stocks so I can do a great job of providing my insight. Salary: Silver.

➢ **Securities and Commodities Trader:** I buy and sell securities and commodities to transfer capital, debt, or risk. I am primarily responsible for determining the terms of sale and negotiating unit prices. Put simply, I connect buyers and seller in the financial markets. Salary: Silver.

Q: What is a Security?

A: A general term for all kinds of financial instruments. It includes stocks, bonds, mutual funds, municipal bonds, etc. Debt securities, also called fixed-income securities, include bonds and Certificate of Deposits (CDs). When you invest your money in a bond, the government or state owes you money and is required to pay you interest. Equity securities are called stocks because you own a part of the company.

Q: What is a Commodity?

A: A basic good used in the world today that people need. These goods can be traded or exchanged for other goods of the same type. The quality is the same across all producers. Here are a few examples:

Softs	Agriculture	Metals	Oilseed	Energy
-Sugar -Cotton -Gur	-Turmeric -Soy bean -Jeera -Chili -Guar Seed	-Gold -Silver -Copper -Aluminum/ Lead -Nickel	-Crude Palm Oil -Mustard Seed -Castor Seed	-Brent Crude -Sweet Crude Oil -Furnace Oil

When stocks and bonds are down, commodities tend to go up. Quick Investment Tip: It is a good idea to include commodities as a part of your portfolio to offset a loss in your investment.

➤ **Venture Capitalist:** I AM an investor in early stage companies. If there is someone who has a great idea for a company, has tested it in the marketplace, and is now able to grow the company, they would come to me for access to capital (money). This capital would allow them to grow the company to the next level. Additionally, I would own a portion of the company because I gave them the money they would need to grow the business. Salary: Silver.

➤ **Hedge Fund – Portfolio Manager:** I use high-risk methods, i.e., investing with borrowed money to maximize my profit potential by investing in highly liquid assets. For example, imagine using $1,000 on your mom's credit card to invest in Facebook. The stock increases dramatically over the next year and your investment is now valued at $10,000. You decide to take out your money before the market crashes and you give you mom back her $1,000. Maybe you give her an extra $500 to cover any interest that accrued on her credit card. You just gained $8,500 and you did not have to use any of your own money. Well, investors do this all the time. Instead of borrowing from their mom, they borrow from the bank or from other people with money. Salary: Platinum.

Beauty: This major industry is centered on making people more beautiful. This industry is valued at $56 billion in the US, as of 2015. Hair care and skin care are two of the largest segments within the beauty industry. Salary varies. Entry Level Salary: Bronze

➤ **Hair Stylist:** I AM excellent at taking care of hair and styling hair.

➤ **Skin Care Specialist:** I help people to have beautiful skin.

➤ **Eye Brow Specialist:** I make sure all my clients have the perfect eyebrows.

Big Data: I work with large data sets and perform in depth analysis to help companies and organizations make sense of data. I am very good at statistics and building mathematical models. Since this is a newer skill set, because of the advent of technology, there is significant opportunity in this space and room for career advancement. Big data has also given me a skill set that I can use in a variety of industries. Salary: Silver.

Broker: I arrange transactions between buyers and sellers for a commission once the deal is fully completed. I can choose the fee that I want to charge and my income is unlimited.

> **High-End Broker:** I have a team of researchers that helps me to study the economy and make predictions about how it will play out. I study the market carefully and help my clients to decide on when to buy or sell a property. Most of my clients are extremely wealthy. Salary varies but it on the higher end. Salary: Titanium

> **Insurance Broker:** I work with different insurance companies to find the right price for my clients (buyers). I ensure that my clients get the best price available on the market and bring business to the insurance companies. I can choose to specialize in health, life, home, auto, or other types. Salary: Bronze.

> **Real Estate Broker:** I AM the intermediary between the buyers and sellers of real estate, real property, and other tangible real estate assets. I find the appropriate match between buyers and sellers and I AM paid a handsome commission to do so. New York and California are my most lucrative markets. Salary: Silver.

> **Stock Broker:** I trade stocks on behalf of my clients who want to invest their money. I complete these trades through a brokerage account. I can be a discount broker where I carry out orders at a discounted commission or a full-service broker where I can fully support and advise my clients. Salary: Bronze.

Business

- ➢ **Management Consultant:** I work with large commercial corporations to help them improve their performance. I work on dynamic, highly talented teams to identify the problems that companies currently have that are preventing them from accomplishing their revenue and growth goals. I provide structured plans for my clients to improve so they can continue to add value in a major way. IT Consulting and Strategy is highly sought after. Salary: Silver.

- ➢ **Government Consultant:** I provide business solutions to government agencies to help them to be more effective at rolling out government programs. I am an expert in my field, often called a subject matter expert, and I work on a small team that shares my area of specialty. Together, we create plans for our clients (government agencies) to improve their performance and help them bring an idea from the research phase to implementation. Salary: Bronze.

- ➢ **Strategy Manager:** I get to oversee a company's plans to develop partnerships with other organizations and teams, drive for growth and expansion, and launch new profit-driven initiatives. Salary: Silver.

- ➢ **Product Manager:** I oversee the product development side of any business. I make sure the correct volume of products is manufactured in a timely manner so that our customers can get their items on time. Salary: Silver.

Additional Options: Beautician, Barber, Baker, Baseball player.

C-suite (Corporate Executives): I basically run the world! Just kidding! But no, really, I oversee some of the largest organizations in the world! Remember those Fortune 100 and Fortune 500 companies we talked about? Well yeah, it is because of my leadership and expertise that it got that big. Do you want to be just like me? On top of the base salary included below, I receive cash bonuses for my performance and equity awards. Salary: Gold.

> **CEO:** Chief Executive Officer – I AM the highest-ranking person in a company or institution and I make managerial decisions. Insurance executives have a huge take home salary exceeding $15 million. Salary: Titanium.[19]

> **COO:** Chief Operating Officer – I AM responsible for overseeing the ongoing business operations within a company. Salary: Silver.

> **CFO:** Chief Financial Officer – I AM responsible for financial planning, record keeping, and reporting to senior management. I manage the financial risks of a company. Salary: Platinum.

> **CLO:** Chief Legal Officer – I help a company minimal their legal risk. I am well versed on all the laws that could affect a company and work to ensure the company obeys the laws to minimize lawsuits. Salary: Platinum.

> **CIO:** Chief Investment Officer – I AM responsible for a company's investment portfolios. Salary: Gold.

> **CTO:** Chief Technology Office - I AM responsible for the scientific and technological issues within a company. Salary: Silver.

Coach

> **Coach:** I work with my clients to help them accomplish their goals and maximize their personal and professional potential. I work with them to identify what is holding them back in the area that they want to see drastic improvement and I function as a catalyst to initiate growth, change, and

---

[19] Chamberlain, Dr. Andrew. "CEO to Worker Pay Ratios: Average CEO Earns 204 Times Median Worker Pay." *Glassdoor.com.* Glassdoor Inc., 25 Aug 2015, Web. 16 Feb 2017.

improvement in their area of focus. I have a specialty area and I stick with it. I can specialize in any of the following: Life Coach, Business Coach, Health Coach, Career Coach, and more. I have my certification from the International Coach Federation. Salary: Silver.

Communications

➢ **Communications Specialist:** I work with companies and individuals to communicate important messages between key stakeholders effectively. Public Relations is a branch of communications as well. Salary: Bronze.

➢ **TV or Radio Talk Show Host:** I have a dapper appearance, articulate speech patterns, and the ability to create a persona that resonates with audiences. According to the U.S. Bureau of Labor Statistics (BLS), "tight broadcast schedules, changes in programming and appearances at public events often require television presenters to work unusual, irregular hours and maintain extremely adaptable schedules and lives." I can study broadcasting, communications, journalism, or a related major to prepare for this career. Salary: $52,000; can have higher income based on one's ability to capture the attention of a large audience. Here are a few talk show hosts with a net worth over a million dollars: Michael Strahan, Kelly Ripa, Robin Roberts, Heidi Klum, Ryan Seacrest ($55 million), Ellen DeGeneres ($75 million), and Dr. Phil McGraw ($88 million).[20]

Computers/Computer Related Careers (See Technology)

➢ **Computer Scientist (Major - Computer Science):** This is an area of study that is the gateway to becoming one of the most valuable members of a team in the 21st century. Computer Science is the study of the principles and use of computers and it is my highest recommendation that students increase their exposure to Computer Science. Consider the major if it is a good fit. You would have one

[20] Crisp, Gavin. "Forbes' 2016 List of the Highest Paid TV Show Hosts." *Etcanada.com.* Corus Entertainment Inc., 6 Oct 2016, Web. 16 Feb 2017.

of the most highly sought after skill sets in the entire world. With this skill, you can build applications, computer programs, websites, and other technological tools that allows companies and organizations to accomplish their missions in innovative ways. Salary: Silver.

➢ **Cloud Computing:** I work with data storage that is not physical but held in a remote location that is called the cloud. I use a network of remote servers hosted on the Internet to store, manage, and process data, rather than a local server or a personal computer. Salary: Silver.

➢ **Cybersecurity:** I AM responsible for keeping everyone's information safe. This includes credit card information, social security numbers, and identification data that is confidential. With the world moving towards so many online transactions, it is important for me to keep the hackers away. Salary: Silver.

Consultant

➢ **Consultant:** I AM an expert in a specific area that I love and I provide advisory services to bring solutions to my clients. Salary varies: Silver.

Construction

➢ **Commercial Manager:** I AM responsible for the financial management of projects, recognizing business opportunities, and putting together bids to win new business. I also negotiate and agree on contracts, which can be worth millions of dollars. Salary: Silver.

➢ **Construction Project Manager:** I oversee a team of construction workers to bring amazing building structures into existence. Sometimes our team gets to knock an entire building down and rebuild it. I plan, organize, supervise, oversee the flow of work, and analyze the logistics of the entire project. I get to manage a $10 million-dollar budget and sometimes even bigger to bring these amazing projects to life. Salary: Bronze.

> **Contracts Manager:** I prepare and review contracts for the purchase or sale of our properties/projects. Salary: Silver.

> **Structural engineer (See Architecture)**

Additional Options: Chef, Counselors, Car mechanic.

Doctor: This career path is all about healing. Doctors will always be needed because there are always people in the world with some sort of ailment who need treatment. Being a doctor is a very secure and rewarding career path. Be prepared for the training that will be required. While this is a 12-year track of getting prepared to be able to save someone's life, it is a very achievable career path once you navigate the training with a strong network around you. You will need four years of undergraduate education, i.e., a bachelor's degree, four years of medical school, i.e., a medical degree, and 2-4 years of residency, i.e., training under another more seasoned doctor.

> **Anesthesiologist:** I make sure that all my patients are safe and well taken care of before, during, and after surgery. I need four years of college, four years of medical school, and four years of residency to be prepared to work with my patients. I will become board certified and I will complete an additional fellowship year of specialty training. Salary: Gold.

> **Dentist:** I make sure your teeth are doing well. Do not forget to brush twice a day and floss every day. Salary: Silver.

> **Family and General Practitioners:** I work with families to make sure they are healthy. Salary: Silver.

> **General Internist:** I work with the prevention, diagnosis, and treatment of adult diseases. Salary: Gold.

➤ **Neurosurgeon:** I specialize in the brain. I am particularly skilled at correcting brain disorders. Salary: Platinum.

➤ **Obstetricians and Gynecologists (OBGYN):** I deliver babies, manage the pregnancy experience for moms, and help to make sure that a female's reproductive organs are healthy. Salary: Gold.

➤ **Occupational Therapy:** I help people with physical, mental, or cognitive injuries to become fully restored. I make sure that they can enjoy life as a normal human being and can do the things that normal people do in their daily lives. I make sure that my patients can participate in the activities of daily living with ease: Bathing, dressing, rest, shopping, meal preparation, etc. Salary: Bronze.

➤ **Optometrist:** I AM an eye specialist. If you have any issues with your eyes, come to me! Salary: Silver.

➤ **Orthodontist:** I AM a more specialized type of dentist that helps people to correct positioning of teeth when the mouth is closed (malocclusion). I deal with overbites and under bites, and other abnormalities. Salary: Gold.

➤ **Oral and Maxillofacial Surgeons:** I specialize in performing surgery on the head, neck, face, jaw (maxillofacial), and mouth (oral). If anyone has a disease, injury, or defect in these areas, they would come to me. Salary: Gold.

➤ **Pediatrician:** I provide preventative health maintenance for children from conception to age 21. I make sure all children are nice and healthy. Salary: Silver

➤ **Physician:** I diagnose and treat injuries or illnesses. Salary: Gold.

> **Podiatrist:** I AM a foot, ankle, and leg specialist. If you break your ankle, I can help! Salary: Silver

> **Prosthodontist:** I develop the teeth people need when their teeth need to be replaced with artificial ones. Providing dentures is one of my specialties. Salary: Silver.

> **Psychiatrist:** I help my patients to heal from mental disorders that may prevent them from living a normal, healthy life. Salary: Silver.

> **Surgeon:** I love operating on people to make them better. I can specialize in many areas. Once I choose an area, I become a master of that area. Salary: Gold.

Director: I AM a senior leader in a company, managing a team or multiple teams to accomplish the goals of an organization. Salary: Silver.

Additional Options: Designers

Economist

> **Economist:** I am an expert on how money and resources are allocated in a country. Salary: Silver.

Educator

> **Education Administrators, Postsecondary:** I AM a leader in the education space, helping to shape the next generation of leaders. I can assume a variety of roles but despite the role, I know I am affecting an entire generation of people. Some roles include, Principal, Vice Principal, Dean, Superintendent, Chancellor, Education Secretary, and more. Salary: Silver

> **Educators:** (see teachers)

Engineer: Engineer build things and are experts at the mechanics behind building complex structures. I will major in engineering when I go to college. I will be good in this field if I have a knack for building things and I maintain a strong foundation in mathematics. Salary: Silver.

➤ **Aerospace engineer:** I AM responsible for evaluating designs to see that the products meet engineering principles. I also design aircraft, spacecraft, satellites, and missiles. When needed, I test prototypes to make sure that they function according to design. I have a bachelor's degree in aeronautical or aerospace engineering. Salary: Silver.

➤ **Architectural & Engineering Manager:** I oversee technical projects. I create project budgets, hire and manage staff, prepare staff training, determine equipment needs, monitor the building and maintenance of equipment, and create detailed plans for reaching technical goals. I have a Master's degree in Engineering Management, Technology Management, or Business Administration. Salary: Silver.

➤ **Chemical engineer:** I apply the principles of chemistry, biology, physics, and mathematics to solve problems that involve the production or use of chemicals, fuel, drugs, food, and many other products. I have a bachelor's degree in chemical engineering. Salary: Silver.

➤ **Computer Hardware Engineer:** I research, design, develop, and test computer systems and components such as processors, circuit boards, memory devices, networks, and routers. I create fast advances in computer technology, by creating new directions in computer hardware. Salary: Silver.

➤ **Drilling Engineer:** I develop, plan, determine the cost of projects, and supervise the operations necessary for drilling oil and gas wells. Salary: Silver.

- **Flight Engineer:** I monitor and operate an airplane's complex aircraft systems. Salary: Silver.

- **Integrated Circuit Designer Engineer:** I provide electrical design and development support to the company I work for or clients I work with. I AM the first person they call to solve technical hardware problems. I will get a Bachelor of Science or Master of Science degree in electrical engineering. Salary varies: Silver.

- **Mining and geological engineer:** I design open-pit and underground **mines**. I also supervise the construction of mineshafts and tunnels in underground operations. Most exciting are the methods that I devise for transporting minerals to processing plants. Salary: Bronze.

- **Nuclear engineer:** I research and develop the processes, instruments, and systems used to derive benefits from nuclear energy and radiation. Sometimes I find interesting ways to use my nuclear research to provide radioactive materials for medical treatment. Salary: Silver.

- **Petroleum Engineer:** After oil is discovered, I work with geologists and other specialists to understand the geologic formation of the rock containing the reservoir. I also determine drilling methods, design and implement the drilling equipment, and monitor operations. I want to work for BP someday! Salary: Silver.

- **Reservoir Engineer:** A branch of petroleum engineering. Salary: Silver.

- **Sales Engineer:** I sell complex scientific and technological products or services to businesses. I have extensive knowledge of the products, parts, and functions and I also understand the scientific processes that make the products work. Salary: Bronze.

Entertainer

> **Actor:** I AM a movie or TV star bringing fictional characters to life through my craft. While this field is highly competitive, the people with the best movies and TV shows have very high take-home pay, e.g., Robert Downing Junior from Iron man earned over $50 million for one Iron man movie. Salary: Bronze - Titanium

> **Comedian:** I make people laugh for a living. I knew I had a gift because people would always crowd around me and laugh at all my jokes. It came naturally to me. It is a grind in the beginning but can be a very rewarding career with a wealth of opportunities. Some of the wealthiest comedian's worth over $100 million include: Larry David, Bill Cosby, Jay Leno, Kevin Hart, Ray Romano, and Steve Harvey. Salary: Bronze - Titanium.

> **Dancer:** I perform a variety of genres before large audiences. Ballet, Jazz, African, Ballroom, etc. Bronze - Titanium.

Entrepreneur: As an entrepreneur, I have unlimited income potential, but I have one of the hardest, most challenging career paths. Aside from being an investor, it is the only other career path that will allow me to make billions. It is very high risk but also very rewarding.

> **Entrepreneur:** I find opportunities to solve problems in the market place by offering a unique and innovative product or service that meets the needs of a target niche. I have unlimited income potential. I develop a skill set around something that is very difficult to do that most people do not know how to do. To be at the top of my game, I work for high-performing, profit-generating companies to learn how a fortune 100 company is run. Then, I leverage these skills to start my own company. When working for a company, I am sure to utilize all training made available, deepen my expertise, and build many great relationships. When the time is right for me to

launch my company, I have all of the resources available to do so. Salary: Unlimited Income Potential, Bronze - Titanium.

Additional Options: Electrician, Editor.

Fashion

➤ **Fabric (Textile) Manufacturer:** I create all kinds of fabric that can be used for clothing, furniture, curtains, bed coverings, hats, and so much more. Salary : Bronze - Titanium. Can be very lucrative based on the number of vendors you provide fabric to.

➤ **Fashion Designer:** I design outfits and clothing for different seasons and occasions. My dream is to have my line of clothing premiered in New York Fashion Week. This would give my brand increased exposure and allow me to work with fabulous models. While this field is highly competitive, the few people who make it become very successful. Salary: Bronze.

➤ **Fashion App Developer:** See Technology

Foreign Languages/Cultures

➤ **Foreign Language Instructor:** I teach people how to speak foreign languages. Salary: Bronze.

➤ **Translator/Interpreter:** I help organizations like the Central Intelligence Agency (CIA), Military, United Nations or Federal Bureau of Investigation (FBI) translate important documents into English so they can better collaborate with foreign countries. I can also work in hospitals to assist with ease of communication between patients and their caregivers. I can also work for technology firms to create products in other languages. There are a plethora of uses for my skill set but I always make it a priority to preserve my secondary and tertiary languages along with my English. Salary: Bronze

Food
> **Head Chef:** I choose all of the menu options provided in a restaurant and manage a team of cooks. Salary: Bronze.

Gaming
> **Game Developer:** I create games for people who love to play them. I AM a software developer or an engineer and I love creating intricate games for people to play. Salary: Bronze.

Geophysicist: I AM a scientist and I use physics, chemistry, geology, and advanced mathematics to study the Earth and its composition. I absolutely loved science in school and wanted to incorporate it into my career. I also get a chance to study the atmosphere's internal make-up, oceans, electrical, and other fields in my work. Salary: Silver.

Goldsmith: I design and make jewelry using gold, silver, precious metals, and precious stones. Once I create the pieces in large numbers, I sell them to retailers all over the world. Salary: Bronze.

Graphic Designer: I create visual concepts that can inspire, inform, or captivate consumers. I design images, flyers, and various promotional material for people, organizations, companies, and programs to help get their message out to the world. There is room for increased earnings once you build a team and develop a scalable model for providing these services. This is true for all freelance or project-based professions. Salary: Bronze.

Green Industry
> **Green Architect/Building:** Energy efficiency is a high priority for the entire world. This is one of the fastest

growing industries and I am so glad that I got into it. Salary: Bronze.

Additional Options: Green Marketers, Gold mining.

Healer

➤ **Dietician/Nutritionist:** I help people eat the right foods and design a food plan that works best for their body and gives them optimal health. Salary: Bronze.

➤ **Doctor:** (see the D section for all types of Doctors)

➤ **Holistic Health Practitioner (Alternative Medicine):** I heal my patients by looking at their whole life and how they interact with their environment to determine how to bring healing and balance to their body. I focus on the body, mind, emotions, and spirit, not just the symptoms. I believe that living a preventative lifestyle is the best way to heal my patients. Salary: Bronze.

➤ **Kinesiology:** I help people to cope with their physical injuries & I work to manage, rehabilitate, and prevent disorders that impede movement. Once I get a master's degree in physical therapy, I can practice my craft at a higher level & can demand a higher salary. Salary: Bronze.

➤ **Occupational Therapy:** I help people with physical, mental, or cognitive injuries to become fully restored. I make sure that they can enjoy life as a normal human being and can do the things that normal people do in their daily lives. I make sure that my patients can participate in the activities of daily living with ease: Bathing, dressing, rest, shopping, meal preparation, etc. Salary: Bronze.

Human Resources

➢ **Compensation & Benefits Manager:** As a compensation manager, I plan, develop, and oversee programs to determine how much an organization pays its employees and how employees are paid. As a benefits manager, I plan, direct, and coordinate retirement plans, health insurance, and other benefits that an organization offers its employees. I have a degree in HR management, industrial psychology, business, or another HR related field. Salary: Silver.

➢ **Human Resources Manager:** I oversee the hiring and firing process for all employees in a firm. I also manage the training and development of all employees. Salary: Silver.

➢ **Training and Development Manager:** I make sure all staff is fully trained and can do their job effectively. I help employees learn new skills and develop existing ones. I also help to design and develop the content taught to employees while assisting my employer to establish the company's needs. Salary: Bronze.

Internet Marketing (See Marketing)

Inventor: I create new products that never existed before, that can help mankind to accomplish tasks better. Elon Musk is a modern day example of an inventor. To build this skill set, I spent a lot of time in robotics, building robots to accomplish tasks; I hang around people with innovative mindsets that know how to think outside the box. Unlimited Income Potential, Salary: Bronze - Titanium

Investments: The wealthiest people in the world are investors. I can invest in any industry as long as I employ the right strategy. Investing is the single best way to become a multi-billionaire. Everyone must master this skill and learn the principles of how to make their money grow.

➢ **Investor:** I seek out opportunities to make my money grow. I make every dollar go to work for me. Each dollar is a little solider and cannot come back home to me without doubling or tripling itself. Revenue varies based on portfolio performance. Salary: Bronze - Titanium

➢ **Investment Banker:** (See banker)

Additional Options: Infrastructure (subway, airplane, trains, roads and highways)

JavaScript

➢ **JavaScript Developer:** I AM responsible for implementing the front-end logic that defines the behavior of the visual elements of a web application. In short, I AM a front-end web developer. Salary: Bronze.

Judge (See Lawyer)

➢ **Judge (Magistrate):** I AM a public official and I have the important responsibility of deciding cases in a court of law. I have a bachelor's degree and a doctor of jurisprudence degree. I successfully passed the bar and was elected to the court to serve in my role. Salary: Silver.

Junior Jobs: These entry-level jobs are where your career may start. In order to secure one of these positions, be sure to fill your resume with internships and other relevant opportunities to make you stand out in the application process. Options: Accountant, Account Executive, Business Analyst, Consultant, Developer, Engineer, and Graphic Designer. Salary: Bronze. Based on the industry and skill-set of choice.

Kinesiotherapist: I provide corrective therapy defined as the application of scientifically based exercise principles adapted to enhance the strength, endurance, and mobility of individuals with functional limitations or those requiring extended physical conditioning. Salary: Bronze.

Knowledge

➢ **Knowledge Management Specialist:** I AM responsible for helping an organization to store and share knowledge across a variety of industries and cross-functional areas. The knowledge may be shared through something called a white-paper. White-papers serve as mini-research papers about specific topics of interest. Make sure you learn about computer applications to be effective in this career path. I AM very valuable to the organization. Salary: Bronze.

➢ **Knowledge Engineer:** I bring together all forms of knowledge into computer systems in order to solve complex problems. Salary: Bronze.

➢ **Thought Leader:** I AM paid for what I know. I am an expert in my field and I position myself as an authority so people, companies, organizations, and schools can learn from my published work. I can package my knowledge in books, textbooks, published papers, and other formats. Unlimited income potential. Based on how knowledge is packaged and marketed. Salary: Bronze – Titanium.

Land Owner (See Real Estate): The most common and fastest way to build wealth is through land ownership. Once you own the land, go ahead and build on it. Everyone should make it a goal to own land within his or her lifetime and pass it down to his or her children. Salary: Titanium

Languages
> **Translator for the CIA or Embassy:** See Translator/Interpreter. Salary: Bronze.

> **Speech Language Pathologist:** I work to prevent, assess, diagnose, and treat speech, language, social communication, cognitive-communication, and swallowing disorders in children and adults. I need a master's degree to practice my profession. Salary: Bronze.

> **Additional Options:** Language consultant (Korean, Arabic, Mandarin, French, Portuguese, Afrikaans, etc.).

Laser Surgeon (See Doctor)

Law
> **Judge:** A judge is a person that makes decisions about whether a person is guilty or innocent. Salary: Silver

> **Judicial Law Clerkship:** I AM an assistant to the judge, and that allows me to gain practical experience and insight about the judicial process by attending judicial proceedings, performing legal research, and supporting the judge with other ad hoc tasks that may present itself. I secured this opportunity right after law school and it is a highly sought after opportunity. Salary: Bronze.

- ➢ **Lawyer:** I know the laws very well and I practice law, as an advocate, barrister, attorney, counselor, solicitor, or chartered legal executive. Salary: Silver.

- ➢ **Law Professor:** I teach law at the college level to train and prepare the next group of lawyers to enter the workforce. Salary: Silver.

Lobbyist
- ➢ **Lobbyist:** I AM charged with the task of influencing the actions, policies, or decisions of government officials and local politicians. I AM very good at the art of persuasion. I know how to sway politicians to vote on legislation in a way that favors the organizations and entities I represent. Salary: Silver.

Makeup Artist
- ➢ **Makeup Artist:** I apply makeup to performers on Broadway, in movies, and on TV shows to reflect the period, setting, and situation of their role. Salary for top 10%: Silver.

Marketing
- ➢ **Brand Manager:** Like a marketing manager, I work to ensure that a brand is successful by performing extensive market research, brand development, and conducting the marketing strategies necessary to get it into the hands of the customer. Salary: Silver.

- ➢ **Creative Director:** I love that I get to bring new marketing initiatives for a company. I get to take the lead on all branding and design related decisions. I am a leader and my creative leadership and ideas get consumers excited about purchasing products and services from the company I support. Salary: Silver.

> **Green Marketer:** I create and implement methods to market green products and services. Salary: Silver.

> **Internet Marketing Specialist:** I use the internet to sell and spread the word about awesome products. I receive payment for each product I sell and I do not have to have a physical location to do it. With the power of the internet, I can access billions of people at any given moment and people can buy products from me while I am sleeping. I love my life! This can serve as an additional stream of income on top of my main gig. Salary: Bronze.

> **Package Design Director:** I design the packages for all the products that go on sale at the stores. Salary: Silver.

> **Graphic Designer:** I create visual projects using computer software or by hand, to communicate a message to a consumer audience. My visual concepts have a goal to inform the customer about the company, inspire the consumer to take action, and captivate the attention of the target audience. Salary: Bronze.

> **Social Media Marketing:** I manage the online presence of a company. I sometimes help promote the websites or projects that a brand is working on and develop social media campaigns to expand visibility. Salary: Bronze.

Management: In any company I work in, I oversee a team of people to accomplish the goals of the organization. I forge strategic partnerships to accomplish mission priorities. I AM very good at keeping my team motivated and focused on the goals of the company and we are very successful at meeting our growth goals. I love this role because it is a transferrable skill set that I can use in a variety of industries. One day, I can become the CEO of the company. Salary: Silver.

> **Types of Managers:** Account Manager, Architectural and Engineering Manager, Business Operations Manager, Computer and Information Systems Manager, Financial

Manager, Hydroelectric Production Manager, Natural Sciences Managers, Pharmacy Manager, Sales Manager (See sales), and Strategy Manager. If interested, reach out to people in these fields for more information. Salary: Silver.

➢ **Gaming Manager:** I plan, direct, or coordinate gaming operations in a casino. I formulate all house rules. Salary of top 10%: Silver, Top-Paying State: NJ.

➢ **Marketing Manager:** I handle all the marketing and advertising for the company I work for. Salary: Silver.

➢ **Mining Manager:** I plan procedures for mining projects, from setting budgets to enforcing deadlines. I have exceptional organizational skills. Salary: Silver.

➢ **Project Manager:** I love managing projects and seeing project goals completed from start to finish. I cannot wait to secure my Six Sigma License. Salary: Bronze.

Media
➢ **Broadcast News Analyst:** I analyze, interpret, and broadcast news received from various sources. I work in Florida, New York, or California. Salary of top 10%: Silver.

➢ **Digital Media Director:** I develop a brand's online presence by implementing effective marketing strategies to drive awareness and increase sales. I AM a master at social media marketing, email marketing, e-commerce, search engine optimization and website traffic. Salary: Silver.

➢ **Newscaster:** I present news during a news program on television, on the radio, or on the Internet. I get to travel quite often to the location where the story is happening. Salary: Bronze, but can bring in seven-figures (Chris Cuomo, Ann Curry, Anderson Cooper, Diane Sawyer, and Katie Couric to name a few).

➤ **Journalist (newspaper):** I gather information and present it in a written or spoken form in news stories, feature articles, or documentaries. I can work for an organization or freelance. Salary: Bronze.

Mathematician

➤ **Actuary:** I analyze financial risk and uncertainty for a company. Salary: Silver.

➤ **Analytics Manager:** I coordinate analytic tasks for the organization I work for, including creating effective strategies to collect data, analyzing information, conducting research, and implementing analytic solutions for their products or services. Salary: Silver.

➤ **Computer and Data Research Scientist/Data Scientist:** I love to solve complex problems in computing. I work with algorithms and try to find mathematical sequences or steps to solve the biggest problems of our time. I helped to end World War II. I want to work for Bloomberg LP one day! Salary: Silver.

➤ **Machine Learning Engineer (Data Scientist):** (See Software Engineer). I build predictive models and apply it to large data sets to identify trends. My skills include computer science, probability and statistics, data modeling and evaluation, software engineering, and system design. Salary: Silver.

➤ **Risk Manager:** I help to put a value on accidents that can potentially happen in the future and hurt a family or company. If my car gets into an accident, there will be money set aside for my car. I work closely with insurance, liability, and legal compliance. Salary: Silver.

➤ **Statistician:** I gather numerical data and then I display the data in a way that can be understood by the average person. I specifically, help companies make sense of quantitative data, spot trends, and make predictions. Salary: Bronze.

Military: I AM responsible for protecting my country from any foreign invaders or international conflict. I can work in a variety of capacities but my primary goal is to lead a large group of soldiers. I plan to attend West Point for the best training and opportunities available. There are five branches of the military: Air Force (air and space protection), Army (on the ground protection), Navy (ocean/sea protection), Marine Corps, and Coast Guard.

  ➤ **Military General:** This is one of the highest positions in the military and is my ultimate goal. Salary: Silver.

Money Manager (See Banker for other business related careers)

  ➤ **Accountant:** I manage the financials for companies and prepare their financial statements. I help to keep track of all the cash flow that comes into an organization and all the money that is owed. I also oversee the company's taxes to make sure they are filing on time. I can start off as a bookkeeper. Salary: Bronze - Silver. Can be much higher depending on industry. Accountants in the finance/tech industry make over six-figures.

  ➤ **Personal Finance Advisor:** I work with individuals to help them to manage their money effectively. I help them set up a budget, an insurance policy, an investment portfolio, and with estate planning to ensure that they are positioned for financial success. Salary: Bronze - Gold.

  ➤ **Tax Manager:** I prepare federal and state income tax returns for individuals, companies, and organizations. I need an accounting degree to be successful in this career track. Salary: Silver.

Music (see various instruments)

  ➤ **Music Publishing Executive:** I AM responsible for ensuring that songwriters and composers receive payment when their compositions are used commercially. I manage the money and the royalties that each song generates. If a songwriter sells their song to me, I become the sole owner of the song and all of the royalties that it generates. If a song is used in a movie, on television, or in a commercial, they must sign contracts with my company for access. Salary: Silver - Titanium

Additional Options: Marine Biologist, Musician.

News Reporter
> ➤ **New Anchor:** I present news during a news program on television, on the radio or on the internet. Salary: Bronze

Non-profit: An organization formed to provide "public benefit" with a focus on maximizing impact instead of maximizing profit. Keep in mind, a non-profit can generate a lot of money and become very profitable. However, all the profit will be reinvested into the company to maximize the impact of the organization. The other benefit to a non-profit is that it is a tax-exempt organization. Tax exempt organizations do not have to pay taxes to the Internal Revenue Service (IRS) at the company level. Gunderson Lutheran Medical Center is a non-profit hospital that brings in over $163 million[21] every year. The Bill and Melinda Gates foundation is a non-profit that brings in $53 billion annually. Big Brother Big Sister brings in over $10 million a year and allocates the funds accordingly. Non-profits can be hospitals, churches, public charities, educational institutions, and social welfare organizations.

> ➤ **Program Director:** I bring a non-profit organization's programs to life by developing a plan of action and carrying out the vision. I organize and manage fundraising events with a focus on budgeting and community outreach. In some cases, I provide grant-writing support to secure additional funds for the organization. Get experience working with a non-profit earlier on to learn how to fulfill this role. Salary: Silver.

---

[21] Lee, Bruce Y. "Very Profitable Nonprofit Hospitals…But Where Are The Profits Going?" *Forbes.com*. Forbes Media, LLC., 8 May 2016, Web. 16 Feb 2017.

Nurturers/Hospital Professions: In a hospital, doctors are the most well trained professionals with 10+ years of training. While they earn a lot of money, the most money is made not through the delivery of care, but from overseeing the business of medicine.

> **Assistant Director of Nursing:** I manage the units in a hospital and hold the staff accountable to ensure they are providing the best quality of service to our patients. I provide performance evaluations to the staff to provide feedback and opportunities for growth. Salary: Silver.

> **Clinical Educator:** I AM an expert in the nursing field and now I help to train the next generation of nurses to be effective in their roles. Salary: Bronze.

> **Doctor:** See doctor.

> **Hospital Administrator:** I oversee the day-to-day operations of a hospital, clinic, managed care organization, or public health agency. I coordinate the actions of all departments in a hospital and ensure they function as one. Salary: Silver.

> **Medical Director:** I AM the top physician leading and director all doctors, nurses, caregivers, and non-medical professionals. I also work with senior leadership to guarantee the medical quality of the hospital. Salary: Gold.

> **Nurse Anesthetist (CRNA):** I take care of patients before, during, and after surgery. I work very closely with the Anesthesiologist. I provide the patients with the medication they need to numb their bodies and go to sleep during surgery. I AM a registered nurse and I have my master's degree. Salary: Silver.

> **Nurse Practitioner (NP):** I collaborate with doctors to give medication. I can do a full physical assessment, write prescriptions, and treat illnesses. I AM a registered **nurse**

(**RN**) with advanced training in diagnosing and treating illness. Salary: Silver.

➤ **Nurse Midwife:** I assist women in all stages of their pregnancy, including pre-natal care, childbirth, and post-delivery. I also work closely with obstetricians and gynecologists (OB-GYN) in diagnosing and treating women with acute and chronic illnesses. Salary: Silver.

➤ **Physician Assistant:** I examine, diagnose, and treat patients under the supervision of a licensed physician. Salary: Silver.

Opportunities

➤ **Opportunities:** This is not a career. However, it is only through opportunities that you will be able to advance your career. It is important that you continue to say the following, "I AM full of access to amazing opportunities and opportunities flow to me easily, frequently, and abundantly. I AM so well connected that many of my opportunities come to me through the people that I know or have access to." You will learn in this world that the quality of your network will determine the magnitude of your success. It is important to be connected to the right people and programs to maximize your access to opportunity. Salary: Invaluable. You are only one connection/opportunity away from becoming a multi-billionaire.

Owner: As you begin to earn money, be sure to turn the money into assets that will help you to build wealth. Ownership is a very important part of career success. It is our responsibility to not just spend all our money but to turn the capital gained into things that will produce wealth for you and your family. Build multigenerational wealth!

> **Owner:** I own so many things and this gives me the freedom to be a leader, manage teams, and change the world through my companies and brands. I play a major role in hiring the people I want to be on my management team. I do not perform physical labor, but I use my money to invest in projects for other people to do the work. I also own stocks and bonds and even books and songs. My family created a line of toothbrushes that turned us into billionaires. My money grows as long as the idea is a good idea and the team is executing the vision effectively. I spend most of my time travelling, connecting with people, and checking in on my investments. I own my own bank. I own an airline. I own my own jets. I own my own hospital. The sky is the limit as long as I have access to capital (money). Everyone can be an owner. Declare: I AM a business owner! Salary: Multi-billionaire, i.e., Carlos Slim. Salary: Titanium

People

> **Engagement Manager:** I help with client relationships. By maintaining relationships with clients, I help to bring in more business to my company. I need to be very good in marketing and project management. Salary: Silver.

> **Design manager:** I envision and execute a customer or client's experience with a company from start to finish. Salary: Silver.

Performer

> **Actor:** I express ideas and portray characters in theater, film, television, and other performing arts media. Salary: Bronze – Titanium, unlimited income potential.

> **Emcee:** Also known as the master of ceremonies. I AM the host at special events and occasions. My most important job is to monitor the agenda carefully to ensure

that the event goes smoothly and according to schedule. Salary: Bronze - Titanium, unlimited income potential.

➤ **Musician:** I perform music for live audiences and recordings. I also audition for positions in orchestras, choruses, bands, and other types of music groups. Lastly, I practice playing instruments or singing to improve my technique so I can be a master at my craft. Salary: Bronze – Titanium, unlimited income potential.

Protection

➤ **Police Officer:** I protect people from harm and crime. Salary: Bronze.

➤ **Detective/Criminal Investigator:** I gather facts for crime investigations. I compile evidence by observing suspects, interviewing witnesses and suspects, and examining physical evidence. Salary: Bronze.

➤ **Special Agent (CIA):** I AM a detective or investigator for a state, county, municipal, federal, or tribal government and I primarily serve in investigatory roles. I work for the FBI. Salary: Silver.

Politician: I AM a representative for the people! I look out for the best interest of the people within my realm of responsibility.

➤ **District Leader:** I represent the members of a political party in my District and ensure that their party is fairly governed by the appointed leaders. I AM a community leader and advocate and I work to ensure that the residents of the district are heard and that their issues are addressed. To get this position, I was elected by my supporters at the party primary. I work with the assembly member in my district to help to accomplish key goals for the people. This is a great stepping-stone for me to move up the political ladder. Unpaid, volunteer based position.

➢ **Assemblyman:** I prepare bills, resolutions, and memorials introduced in the General Assembly. Salary varies by state. NY Salary: Bronze.

➢ **City Councilman:** I represent specific districts within a state. Salary: Silver.

➢ **Comptroller:** I AM the state's chief accountant or financial officer. I oversee the state budget and the tax dollars to ensure the money is spent appropriately. I pay state employees and oversee their pension funds. I prepare financial reports, examine government contracts, and collect taxes to fund state programs. I have an accounting degree (or finance degree) and a great deal of experience working with large budgets. Salary: Bronze.

➢ **Governor:** I oversee all professionals who work for the state and make sure they are performing at optimal levels. I can veto state bills (laws) that the legislature passes. I can decide how funds are allocated across the entire state. I AM the highest elected official in my state and I lead my political party. I represent my state in meetings and have an obligation to let the citizens know how the state is doing. Salary: Silver.

➢ **Political Scientist:** I work to understand the science of politics and to understand the types of dynamics that are at play. Salary: Silver.

➢ **President of the United States (POTUS):** I AM responsible for establishing treaties or agreements with other nations concerning trading terms and the aid that the United States gives to needy countries. I also appoint ambassadors to represent the United States in foreign countries. I AM the Commander in Chief of the armed forces. Salary: Platinum.

➢ **Senator:** I represent the people living in my state in the Senate. I write and vote on new laws called "bills." Salary: Silver.

➢ **House of Representative:** I make and pass federal laws. Salary: Silver.

Note: Congress is made up of the Senate and the House of Representatives.

Prosthetist: I design and fit prosthetic limbs for medical patients with body deformities and disorders. I examine the affected area for factors that could impact the fitting of the prosthetic device along with the placement of it. Salary: Bronze

Prosthetic Technician: I use machinery and computer equipment to design, create and customize prosthetic limbs made of wood, metal, or plastic. The end product is covered in rubber or latex and is most often painted a color similar to that of my patients' skin to make the device look more natural. Salary: Lower Bronze.

Public Relations Executive: I AM responsible for managing the image of people, companies, and brands. I help to paint them, in the media, in a positive light and provide increased exposure for what they do. Salary: Gold.

Additional Options: Paleontologist, Penny Stock Trader, Personal Trainer, Pharmacist, Photographer, Plumber, Publisher, Psychologist.

Quality

➢ **Quality Assurance Manager:** I AM very good at assessing what the customer requires out of a final deliverable and ensuring that my team meets all requirements down to the last detail. I determine, negotiate, and agree on in-house quality procedures, standards, and specifications. Salary: Silver.

➤ **Quality Control Analyst:** I work under the quality assurance manager and I carry out all of the requested tasks. I will do a great job so I can move up the ranks. Salary: Bronze.

Quarry

➤ **Quarry Manager:** I help to extract stone or other materials from the earth. Salary: Silver.

Quartermaster

➤ **Quartermaster:** I steer ships and maintain visual communications with other ships. I steer ships under the direction of the ship's commander, navigating officer, or direct helmsman to steer, following designated course. Salary: Lower Bronze.

Additional Options: Quantum Physicist.

Real Estate

➤ **Flipping Houses**: I AM a real estate investor and I purchase homes at an auction for a cheap price and resell them at a significant profit months down the road. Houses go to auction when a family can no longer afford to pay the mortgage. The bank takes it over and sells it to the highest bidder at an auction. The more houses I flip, the more I earn. I can earn around $30,000 - $60,000 for each house that I flip. Salary: Platinum - Titanium.

➤ **Real Estate Broker:** I receive a commission for connecting the buyer or renter of a property to the seller. In the right market, the salary can be over 6-figures (New York or California). Salary: Bronze - Silver.

➢ **Real Estate Investor:** I purchase a property on my own or pool my money together with other buyers to make an investment in a property. This money is used to make repairs and improvements to the property. Once the property is improved, I sell the property at a much higher price and receive a major profit. I return an agreed upon percentage to the investors in my fund. Even if I make a 40% profit, if I only agreed to return 20% to the investors, that is all I am obligated to provide. Salary: Silver - Titanium.

Research

➢ **Equity Research Analyst:** I research all the stocks trading on the stock market and make decisions about whether to buy, sell, or hold a particular stock. I typically specialize in a particular sector to become an expert at it and really study the trends of the market. Salary: Silver.

➢ **Research Analyst:** I perform extensive research for companies to help them make decisions about future projects, products, contracts, and company growth opportunities. Salary (Market Research Analyst): Bronze. Salary (Operations Research Analyst): Bronze - Silver.

➢ **Research & Development:** I get to do the coolest research on new products that my company would like to bring to the marketplace. I also get to research how to improve on the design of a product that currently exists. Salary: Bronze.

Robotics

➢ **Robotics Engineer:** I build robots to make life easier for myself, my family, my school, and people all over the world. Imagine building a robot that could clean your room for you. Wouldn't that be awesome! Robots can be very helpful to society and me. Salary: Silver.

Sales

➢ **Sales Associate:** I sell all kinds of things for companies and I receive a commission on each sale. I sell iPads, laptops, insurance, basketballs, textbooks, tablets, food, and so much more to increase revenue for the company. Commission Based, high earning potential. Salary: Silver – Platinum.

➢ **Sales Manager:** I AM responsible for leading and guiding a team of sales people in an organization. I set sales goals & quotas, build a sales plan, analyze data, assign sales training and sales territories, mentor the members of my sales team, and am involved in the hiring and firing process. I travel all over the world to do my job well and meet with my teams. I have a bachelor's degree in business administration and/or marketing. I was sure to take courses in economics, finance, accounting, business law, and statistics to be able to excel in my field. Salary: Silver.

Solar

➢ **Solar Energy:** I use the sun to bring energy to homes, offices, buildings, and other facilities. I create the devices that people can use to run their operations. Salary: Bronze - Silver. Provide innovative solutions and take on a leadership role to maximize your income opportunities.

Science

➢ **Biochemist/Molecular Biologist:** I AM an expert at chemical processes that occur within living organisms. I can work anywhere in the US and for a wide variety of industries from manufacturing, farming, or oil and gas. I can work in hospitals, labs, research facilities, biotechnology (biotech) firms, clinics, pharmaceutical companies, and so many more. I had lots of lab and research experience in college along with two internships to stand out when I interviewed for full time roles. Salary: Silver.

> **Forensic Scientist:** I help investigate crimes by collecting and analyzing physical evidence. I can choose two tracks in my career path: crime scene investigation or laboratory analysis. Salary: Bronze.

> **Geophysicist:** I AM a scientist and I use physics, chemistry, geology, and advanced mathematics to study the Earth and its composition. I absolutely loved science in school and wanted to incorporate it into my career. I also get a chance to study the atmosphere, internal make-up, oceans, electrical, and other fields in my work. Salary: Silver.

> **Material Scientist:** I research and study the structures and chemical properties of various natural, synthetic, or composite materials. This includes metals, alloys, rubber, ceramics, semiconductors, polymers, and glass. In the solar power industry, I study solar cells to enhance the technology and create new products. Salary: Bronze.

> **Pharmacist:** I work with health care teams to bring patients the best drugs needed to make them better. I make sure my patients receive the correct prescription and I coach them on how to use the prescriptions safely. I have a strong chemistry background and a deep understanding of the biomedical. I need a Doctor of Pharmacy to become a pharmacist, which will take me four years. I also have to pass two exams to get my license. Salary: Silver.

> **Physicist:** I explore how things move and the mechanics behind it. I study matter and energy across the physical universe. I have a B.S. in physics and have mastered calculus so I made sure I did well in all my math classes. I have a Masters or PhD in physics so I can work on cool research and explore new discoveries. Salary: Silver.

Sea

➢ **Captain, Mates, and Pilots of Water Vessels:** I steer a ship to help to get people from one place to another on the water. I work in Rhode Island most often. Salary of top 10%: Silver.

Speaker

➢ **Motivational Speaker:** I AM a special type of public speaker that delivers speeches that inspire and motivate large audiences. Salary: Bronze – Titanium.

➢ **Public Speaker:** I AM an expert at communicating information to large audiences. Toastmasters is an excellent club to join to sharpen this skill. Salary can vary. Speakers can earn anywhere from $500 - $100,000 per speaking engagement. Salary: Bronze – Titanium.

Spirituality

➢ **Theologian:** I AM an expert on the Christian faith and I conduct research, teach, and write about Christianity. I was called to the ministry of theology. Salary: Bronze.

➢ **Minister (Pastor):** I work with the elders in a church to oversee the growth and direction of the church. I have a solid handle on the purpose, values, and strategy of the church and am highly skilled in assigning appropriate roles and responsibilities to ordained and lay staff. Salary: Bronze.

Sports

➢ **Physical Therapist:** I help injured/ill people improve their movement and manage their pain. Salary: Bronze.

Survivor Skills Expert

➢ **Agricultural Specialist:** I provide expertise in agricultural matters, laws, and regulations and make recommendations concerning best practices, equipment, or actions to organizations and individuals. Salary: Bronze.
  ✓ Bunkers (Underground homes)

✓ Farmers (See Agriculture)
✓ Food preparation/Food storage

Additional Options: Sanitation Worker, Social Worker.

Teacher

➢ **Professor (see Educators for more information):** I can teach my area of specialty, like engineering, law, business, solar energy, English, clinical education, mathematics, etc. to college students or higher to help build the next generation of leaders. Most of my job is centered around producing ground-breaking research to move the world forward and make my university look good. I can also be a consultant or content writer. Once I achieve tenure at my university, I will have a protected job for the rest of my career. Salary: Silver.

Technology: Technology is all over the world. It is pervasive. With this skill set, I can work with any industry. The more skills I gain, the more value I provide, the more I earn.

➢ **Big Data:** I create and manage extremely large data sets that are highly complex. Not even traditional data processing applications are adequate to handle them. (See Big Data). Salary: Silver.

➢ **Ethical Hacker:** I have the fun job of hacking into computer systems and it is legal. They call me a white-hat. Salary: Bronze.

➢ **Software Developer, Applications (Apps):** I develop software applications for all kinds of software using JavaScript, C++, or ORACLE. I can work in a variety of industries. If I bring industry knowledge to the table as well, I AM more valuable. There are no limits. Salary: Bronze.

➤ **Software Architect/Application Systems Architect:** I love creating computer programs and communicating these technical plans to the leaders of the companies, I work with. Salary: Silver.

➤ **Software Development Manager:** I get to develop and oversee the systems behind computer programs to make sure it runs efficiently without glitches. Salary: Silver.

➤ **Systems/Data Architect:** I create information and technology road maps for a company. I have a degree in computer science or information systems. Salary: Silver.

➤ **Information Technology (IT) Manager:** I make sure that all of my company's equipment, software, and networks operate smoothly and execute the IT goals of the organization. I have my bachelor's degree in information technology and have many technical skills as well. Salary: Silver.

Typist
➤ **Typist:** I AM a master typist and can type 200 words a minute. I use my skill as a court reporter, broadcast captioning and real-time reporting for Web casts. Salary: Silver in certain cities.

Additional Options: Travel Agent

Undertaker: Also known as a mortician or funeral director. I work in and with funeral homes to provide funeral and embalming services for the dead and their families. Salary: Bronze.

Underwriter

> **Bank Loan Underwriter:** I review a person's credit history to determine the likelihood that a bank will give them a loan. I calculate financial risks & losses. Salary: Bronze.

> **Insurance Underwriter:** I analyze risk in insurance proposals to protect the company for which I work. I also determine policy terms and calculate premiums based on actuarial, statistical, and background information. I have excellent communication and negotiation skills and I AM highly analytical. Salary: Bronze.

University Relations Manager: I provide day-to-day client management for a company's school partners. I serve as the daily point of contact with university partners, as well as collaborate with the University Relations team to support the expansion needs in established markets. Salary: Bronze.

Urban/Regional Planning: I develop land, using plans and programs that help create communities, accommodate population growth, and revitalize physical facilities in towns, cities, counties, and metropolitan areas. Salary: Bronze.

User Experience Designer (Ui/UX Designer): I understand technology, business goals, and the psychology of the consumer. My main duty is to conduct user research, interviews, & surveys. Once I gather this valuable information, I use it to create sitemaps, wireframes, and prototypes that would best meet the desires of the user. In other words, I help to create user-friendly, online experiences for brands. Salary: Bronze.

Vehicles

> **Auto Mechanic:** I fix cars for a living. I AM very good at finding the parts that are malfunctioning in a car, bus, truck, or other automobile and I bring it up to a usable standard.

As the owner of an auto repair shop, I can make over six-figures. Salary: Lower Bronze.

> **Additional Options:** Flying Car manufacturer/inventor.

Vice President: I AM second in command in the public or private sector, overseeing the overall business, organization, agency, institution, union, university, government, country, or branch of government. I report to the President or CEO and can also head up divisions within a company. Salary: Silver.

Videographer: I shoot video footage and assist in editing. I perform most of the tasks related to production and post-production. Salary: Bronze.

Videogame Designer: I create the best video games that everyone loves to play. I choose the characters, the special effects, the colors, and decide on the various levels a gamer will move through to advance towards victory. Salary: Bronze.

Veterinarian: As long as there are farm animals, there will be a demand for my work. The U.S. Department of Agriculture's One Health approach emphasizes the idea that the health of animals is intimately connected to human & environmental health. Salary: Silver.

Violinist (See music).

Wind Energy: Wind turbines convert the kinetic energy in the wind into mechanical power. This mechanical power can be used for specific tasks (such as grinding grain or pumping water) or a generator can convert this mechanical power into electricity to power homes, businesses, schools, and the like.[22] I love this emerging field

---

[22] "Wind Energy Basics" *windeis.anl.gov.* Bureau of Land Management, n.d., Web. 26 Feb 2017.

because it is growing very fast. People all over the world are looking to wind as a new source of energy to preserve the earth. There are a variety of roles available including: engineer, operations manager and project Manager. Salary: Silver.

Wine Taster:
  ➢ **Master Sommelier:** I AM a wine connoisseur and I work with restaurants to appropriately pair food with the right wine. I have a great personality, I lead and direct others and I AM an excellent communicator. I interact with people from different backgrounds. Salary: Silver

Writer
  ➢ **Author:** I write books, articles, and reports for different audiences. Salary: Bronze.

  ➢ **Blogger:** I write about a topic that is of interest to me consistently and frequently. As my audience grows, companies that want to advertise their products on my websites so they can reach my audience pay me. I can choose a topic about health, money, finance, education, recreational activities, dating and relationships, and so much more. I can do this part time to supplement my income. Salary: Bronze.

  ➢ **Editor:** I plan, coordinate, and revise material for publication in books, newspapers, magazine, or websites. I can be a freelancer as well. Salary: Bronze.

  ➢ **Journalist:** I research and gather information about relevant topics in present day society at major events and occurrences that the public wants to know about it. Once I collect the information, I write and present the content to the world. I AM an excellent communicator and highly skilled at presenting information. Salary: Bronze.

  ➢ **Technical Writer:** I write technical materials, such as equipment manuals, appendices, or operating and maintenance instructions. I also assist in layout work. Salary of top 10%: Silver. Top-paying state: California.

Additional Options: Water Resource Specialist, Wellness Instructor, Wholesale and Manufacturing.

X-Ray Technician: I use machines to produce medical images of a patient's body. These images give other health care professionals information to help diagnose or prescribe treatment for a patient. Salary: Bronze.

Xenobiologist: I study extraterrestrial life forms. I have a masters or PhD in physics or astronomy. Salary: Silver.

Xml Developer (Also known as Extensible Markup Language): I work with this markup language to define a set of rules for encoding documents easily. (See Software Developer). Salary: Silver.

Yacht Broker: I sell luxury boats to the wealthy. I AM a specialist who functions as the intermediary between the buyer and the seller of yachts. Salary: Silver.

Yard Manager: I supervise and coordinate activities of workers engaged in loading, transferring, and operating trains and locomotives in an industrial yard. Salary: Bronze.

Youth and Children Program Director (See non-profit): I AM a youth program director. I help young people achieve their biggest dreams and accomplish their goals through structured programming. I plan, organize, and manage fundraising events with a focus on budgeting and community outreach. Salary: Silver.

Zoning Manager
➤ **Real Estate Zoning Manager:** I work in the real estate sector and I oversee the municipality's land-use codes and bylaws, the coordination of enforcement efforts, and the promotion of zoning information. I am an expert at urban planning. I have a bachelor's or master's degree in urban planning or a related field. Salary: Silver.

Zoologist
➤ **Zoologist:** I study animals and other wildlife and how they interact with their ecosystem. I also research the development of animal diseases. I am well versed on the entire animal kingdom and I study the physiology of animals and their behavior. Salary: Bronze.

Zumba
➤ **Zumba Dance Instructor (See Wellness):** I teach a Colombian dance fitness program, created by Alberto "Beto" Perez, to make working out more fun. I teach classes all over the world and people enjoy working out with me because I make it worth their while. Salary: Bronze

➤ **Zumba Dance Owner:** I AM the creator, creative director, and part owner of Zumba! I AM Alberto "Beto" Perez. Net Worth: $30 million.

17. THE STRUCTURE OF A COMPANY

Your goal in any company you work for is to move up the ranks within the organization. While the organizational structure of every company may be a little different, you should still focus on advancement. Use this chart to explore the positions within a sample company's organizational structure. Start learning and researching how to move up the ranks in any company for which you work. These are important questions to ask early on in your career. Start exploring the level of responsibility that is required of a supervisor, manager, director, vice president, or c-suite employee. Research the type of leadership roles you can assume right now to learn how to lead and inspire people into action. Keep your eye on the prize. The focus is on being a part of senior leadership. Repeat after me: I run the world!

Sample Organizational Structure

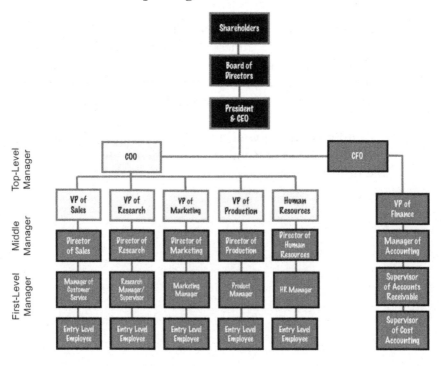

18. NEXT STEPS

Knowledge is only useful when applied. That's right, you have just filled your brain with high-quality knowledge. Now, you need to take action! You have learned a great deal of information about your dream career and have learned a few details about what the career path will require. I challenge you to develop **three** immediate next steps that you will take **right now** to give you a jump-start on your new career journey and WRITE IT DOWN! Do not waste any time. The time is now and you do not want to lose the momentum that you already have. Get an accountability partner. It could be your parents, a sibling, or a good friend. Make sure you share these three goals with them and you give yourself a timeline to get it done. Your timeline can be any of the following: 1 week, 2 weeks, 1 month, or 3 months. Check in to ensure that you are progressing toward your goal.

	Description	Timeline
Goal #1		
Goal #2		
Goal #3		

19. THE END. BUT REALLY, THE BEGINNING

I hope you have enjoyed exploring these career options. Take some time to study all of them. I can assure you, it will give you a better understanding of how the world works. Our world is changing very fast! There will be a plethora of opportunities to work on interdisciplinary teams. The person who has a broad understanding of how the world works and has insight into a few different industries or skill sets will be in a better position to add value to any team they work with. Make yourself stand out by expanding your awareness of what is out there for you.

Secondly, you will notice that many of the careers that pay the most are leadership positions. Develop your leadership and public speaking skills from a very early age. I would start this from upper elementary school (age 8+). All children should be well-trained public speakers. By middle school, begin to foster your ability to lead a small team of people to accomplish a goal.

Thirdly, be sure to make it your business to innovate. It is the responsibility of Generation Y and Generation Z to create the jobs of tomorrow because many of the current jobs will not exist due to the growth of technology and something called automation. Make it your top priority to bring new and fresh ideas to the table on how to solve the world's biggest problems and be bold enough to get out there and build viable solutions that can make a difference. A mindset of innovation can be developed while you are in school. When you see a problem in your school, do you complain about it or do you think of a solution, present it to your school administrators and make it your business to implement it? Innovation is a way of life that can be mastered from an early age.

I would like to leave you with one final suggestion to remain competitive as we move towards a globalized economy and technology continues to become pervasive. Due to the rapidly changing world and the technology age, there are four areas you should become highly adept at: science, mathematics, engineering, and economics. Bill Gates said it best, "Workers proficient in these areas will be the agents of change for all institutions." Do not take this advice lightly. These four areas will turn you into a master problem solver and will make you an asset to the organization you decide to work for. Therefore, get straight A's in all of your classes and pay closer attention to your math and science classes so you are in the best position possible to earn lots of money and have lots of impact later on. For those who do not love math and science, all is not lost. Become an expert in your chosen field and reference the 'Skills Worth Mastering' list to see how you can find a skill within the realm of your passion that is marketable.

Cheers to the start of a wonderful career and a chance for you to dream big and put some action behind those career aspirations. Seek out mentorship and internships from people in your chosen field and you are sure to win. Use your words to speak your biggest desires into your life. For example, "I AM a Yale graduate with a degree in biology. I AM a neurosurgeon and motivational speaker. I AM fully funded for my schooling." Always remember to do what you love and what you do well (your strength/gifts) and you will thrive. Become a master at your craft (approximately 10,000 hours according to Malcom Gladwell) and rise all the way to the top! The world is waiting for your brilliance. I am expecting your excellence! It is your destiny to be successful. So, the next time someone asks you the most commonly asked question, "Who are you?" and you go on to ask yourself, "Who I am?" before responding, I want you to declare to that someone, loud and clear that, "I AM the light of the world and have been placed on this earth for a reason. I AM excelling in my craft because I have found my "sweet spot" and I stick to it. I AM focused, disciplined, capable, reliable, and excelling. I know that anything I touch will prosper so I move forward, audaciously in the direction of my biggest dreams. I AM the head and not the tail. I AM a leader and not a follower. I AM on my journey to discover my purpose and I AM getting closer and closer every day. Amid my journey, I AM clear about who I AM and I walk this earth with confidence, dignity, and faith. I AM somebody who will use my gifts to change the world and I AM boldly walking in my divine destiny."

From: Your mentor and success coach
With loads of love,
Tai Abrams

STAY FOCUSED | STAY DRIVEN
Now, step into your divine destiny

RECOMMENDED RESOURCES

ADDITIONAL READING

1. 1001 Ways to Pay for College by Gen and Kelly Tanabe
2. Gruber's Complete SAT Guide 2015 by Gary R. Gruber, Phd
3. From Good to Great by James C. Collins
4. The Money Mastery Project by Tai Abrams (Coming Soon)
5. What Color is Your Parachute? A Practical Manual for Job-Hunters and Career-Changers by Richard N. Bolles
6. Strengths Finder 2.0 by Tom Rath
7. The Pathfinder: How to Choose or Change Your Career for a Lifetime of Satisfaction and Success by Nicholas Lore
8. Getting from College to Career by Lindsey Pollak
9. Careers: The Graphic Guide to Finding the Perfect Job for You by DK

WEBSITES TO CHECK OUT

1. www.DoSomething.org
2. www.Glassdoor.com
3. www.Salary.com
4. www.PayScale.com
5. www.Meetup.com
6. www.Indeed.com
7. www.Linkedin.com
8. www.Truity.com
9. www.Vault.com
10. www.Economist.com
11. www.ft.com
12. www.CareerBuilder.com
13. www.InsideJobs.com
14. www.GeneralAssemb.ly

Career Affirmations to Help You Walk in Your Divine Purpose and Find the Career You Love

Who is the most important person to you in the whole wide world?
I AM.

Use these words to paint your ideal reality. Your words are your
magic wand. Say these affirmations 100 times a day.

I AM the director of my career.
I take the initiative to have the career of my dreams.
I AM a genius. I AM enthusiastic. I AM abundant. I AM capable.
I AM confident. I AM detail-oriented. I AM consistent. I AM wonderful.
I AM productive. I achieve mastery. I AM marketable. I AM highly-skilled.
I impress the world. I take calculated risks. I finish what I start.
I AM a disruptive leader. I AM victorious. I AM valuable.
Every no gets me closer to a yes!
I AM successful in my interviews.
I have a bright future ahead of me.
The right doors are opening for me.
I AM deeply fulfilled by all that I do.
I bring great energy everywhere I go.
My divine destiny is now fulfilled in my life.
I follow through with what I say I am going to do.
I love the work that I do, and I am well paid for it.
The favor of God surrounds me today like a shield.
I AM appreciated and well compensated wherever I work.
I love my career and I amaze people with my exceptional results.
I always work for wonderful bosses who challenge me to be great.
Amazing opportunities constantly show up in my life miraculously.
My purpose is found when I use my talents to help a lot of people.
I deserve to have this exciting, rewarding career. It is so much fun.
I AM an asset to any organization and I prove it in my interview.
All the people, opportunities, resources, money and ideas are
showing up for me right now in miraculous ways.
My job allows me to express my talents and abilities,
and I am grateful for this employment.
I nail every interview I go on and I AM
constantly hired on the spot with a signing bonus.
When it is time for a new job, the perfect position presents itself easily.

REFERENCES

Becraft, Michael B. *Bill Gates: A Biography*. Santa Barbara: ABC-CLIO, LLC, 2014. Print.

Berman, Dan. "30 Worst Paying College Majors: 2016." *ALM Media, LLC*, 11 May 2016, http://www.thinkadvisor.com/ 2016/05/11/30-worst-paying-college-majors-2016. Accessed15 Mar. 2017.

Bort, Julie. "If you want to be a millionaire, it's better to be a software engineer than a pro athlete." *Business Insider*, 5 Feb. 2017, http://www.businessinsider.com/better-to-be-a-software-engineer-than-a-pro-athlete-2017-1?utm_content=buffer089d8&utm_medium=social&utm_source=facebook.com&utm_campaign=buffer-ti. Accessed 7 Apr. 2017.

Bureau of Labor Statistics. *Occupational Employment Statistics*. United States Department of Labor, 31 Mar. 2017, www.bls.gov/oes/current/oes_stru.htm/. Accessed 7 Apr. 2017.

Chamberlain, Dr. Andrew. "CEO to Worker Pay Ratios: Average CEO Earns 204 Times Median Worker Pay." *Glassdoor*, 25 Aug. 2015, www.glassdoor.com/research/ceo-pay-ratio. Accessed 28 Feb. 2017.

Chappell, Joe. "What is the Average Global C-Suite Executive Salary?" *Blue Steps*, 10 Oct. 2012, www.bluesteps.com/blog/what-is-the-average-global-c-suite-executive-salary.aspx. Accessed 1 Mar. 2017.

Columbus, Louis. "Where Big Data Jobs Will Be In 2015." *Forbes*, 29 Dec. 2014, www.forbes.com/sites/louiscolumbus/2014/12/29/where-big-data-jobs-will-be-in-2015/#13204c7c404a. Accessed 28 Feb 2017.

Comm, Joel. "How This 17-Year-Old Genius Is Making More Than $30,000 Each Month on the Internet." *Inc.com*, 21 Jan. 2016, www.inc.com/joel-comm/how-this-17-year-old-genius-is-making-over-$30000-each-month-on-the-internet.html. Accessed 28 Feb 2017.

Dice. "2015 – 2016 Dice Salary Survey." *Dice.com*, 26 Jan. 2016, http://marketing.dice.com/pdf/Dice_TechSalarySurvey_2016.pdf. Accessed 7 Feb. 2017.

Dill, Kathryn. "The Highest-Paying Tech Jobs Right Now." *Forbes*, 22 Apr. 2016, www.forbes.com/sites/kathryndill/2016/04/22/the-highest-paying-tech-jobs-right-now/#63483cc4257a. Accessed 28 Feb 2017.

Gladwell, Malcolm. *Outliers: The Story of Success*. New York: Little, Brown and Company, 2008. Print.

Hay, Louise. *I Can Do It: How to Use Affirmations to Change Your Life*. Carlsbad: Hay House, Inc, 2004.Print.

Jordan, Gabrielle. The Making of a Young Entrepreneur. Bowie: Legacy Builder Group, 2011. Print.

Made in America. Dir. Ron Howard. Prod. Ron Howard and Brian Grazer. Phase 4 Films, 2013. Film.

Miller, Fred E. *No Sweat Elevator Speech!: How to craft your elevator speech, floor by floor, with no sweat!* St. Louis: Fred Co., 2014. Print.

Palmer, Parker J. *Let Your Life Speak: Listening for the Voice of Vocation*. San Francisco: Jossey-Bass, 1999. Print.

Renzulli, Kerri Anne, et al. "The 21 Most Valuable Career Skills Now." *Time*, 16 May 2016, time.com/money/4328180/most-valuable-career-skills. Accessed 7 March 2017.

Scheidies, Nick & Tart, Nick. "Mark Bao Interview: 11 Companies and 3 Foundations by Age 17." JuniorBiz, n.d., http://juniorbiz.com/interview- mark-bao. Accessed 7 March 2017.

Smith, Jacquelyn. "The 30 Highest-Paying Jobs in America." *Business Insider*, 23 Sep. 2015, www.businessinsider.com/top-paying-jobs-in-america-2015-9. Accessed 7 Apr. 2017.

"The 37 Highest-Paying Jobs in America." *Business Insider*, 19 Aug. 2016, www.businessinsider.com/highest-paying-jobs-in-america-2016-8. Accessed 7 Feb. 2017.

The Holy Bible, King James Version. Cambridge Edition: 1769; *King James Bible Online*, 2017. www.kingjamesbibleonline.org.

"Too Much of a Good Thing." *The Economist*, 26 Mar. 2016. *The Economist*. Web. Accessed 9 May 2017.

Tracy, Brian. *The Gift of Self-Confidence*. India: Jaico Publishing House, 1998. Kindle.

The Power of Self Confidence: Become Unstoppable, Irresistible, and Unafraid in Every Area of Your Life. Hoboken: John Wiley & Sons, Inc., 2012. Print.

U.S. Department of Labor, Bureau of Labor Statistics. *Occupational Outlook Handbook, 2014-15*. 17 Dec 2015. Web. 21 Mar 2017. <https://www.bls.gov/ooh/home.htm>.

Voogd, Peter. *6 Months to 6 Figures*. USA: Game Changers Inc., 2016. Print.

Ward, Marguerite. "The 25 Highest-Paying Jobs in America." *CNBC*, 26 Jul. 2016, www.cnbc.com/2016/07/26/the-25-highest-paying-jobs-in-america.html. Accessed 15 Mar. 2017.

"Bill Gates Says People with these 3 Skills Will Be Successful in the Future Job Market." *CNBC*, 22 Dec. 2016,**www.cnbc.com/2016/12/22**/bill-gates-says-people-with-these-3-skills-will-be-successful-in-the-future-job-market.html. Accessed 15 Mar. 2017.

ABOUT THE AUTHOR

Duke graduate and edupreneur, Tai Abrams is on a mission to establish an education to wealth pipeline where children have the tools they need to excel in school, gain admission into top schools, secure lucrative careers and leverage the money earned to build multigenerational wealth. As the founder and CEO of AdmissionSquad, Inc., her program has helped talented middle schoolers gain admission into NYC's top high schools, with an 80% success rate. Alumni of her program have gained admission into schools like Kent, Stuyvesant, Bard, Brooklyn Tech, Packer Collegiate, NEST+m and many more. Tai believes our life's work is to reach our highest potential, so she helps teens start the success journey as early as possible, to help them experience the kind of success that brings them true joy. She believes that the biggest barrier to accessing one's true potential is the lack of knowledge necessary to get there. Much of her work is centered around bridging the information gap facing students and their parents as they navigate the American education system and begin the career exploration process.

Tai graduated with an Advanced Regents Diploma from The Bronx High School of Science and a Bachelor of Arts in mathematics from Duke University. Blessed with a knack for working with numbers, she has used her gifts to make math & money mastery easy for children and adults in many places, including the United States, Barbados, Egypt, South Africa, and more. Tai is available for personal appearances, seminars, and book signings on a limited basis. She brings her insights, talents, and expertise to schools, organizations, churches, and corporate offices in the form of high quality, engaging, and life transforming workshops. She would love to hear from you. Stay in touch!

Visit TaiAbrams.com for more information.

Email: info@TaiAbrams.com Facebook & Instagram: @IamTaiAbrams

NOTES

Made in the USA
Monee, IL
12 June 2020